EDITING
THE MIDDLE ENGLISH
MANUSCRIPT

EDITING THE MIDDLE ENGLISH MANUSCRIPT

Charles Moorman

UNIVERSITY PRESS OF MISSISSIPPI
Jackson
1975

Copyright © 1975 by the
University Press of Mississippi
Library of Congress Catalog Card Number 74–17511
ISBN 0–87805–063–9
Manufactured in the United States of America
Designed by J. Barney McKee

THIS VOLUME IS AUTHORIZED
AND SPONSORED BY THE
UNIVERSITY OF SOUTHERN MISSISSIPPI
HATTIESBURG, MISSISSIPPI

CONTENTS

ACKNOWLEDGMENTS

As ALWAYS, I am beholden to others for whatever of worth this book contains and can blame only myself for its faults.

The long extract from *The Works of Geoffrey Chaucer*, 2nd edition, edited by F. N. Robinson, copyright © 1957 by Houghton Mifflin Company is used by permission of the publishers.

I have as usual shamelessly taken advantage of the generosity of the President of the University of Southern Mississippi, William D. McCain.

I am indebted to George Pace, to J. Barney McKee, and to Mrs. Catherine Rhodes Adams, all of whom managed to salvage the manuscript from most of my errors and attempts at humor.

My greatest debt as always is to my wife, who could have written a better book than I and should have.

EDITING
THE MIDDLE ENGLISH
MANUSCRIPT

INTRODUCTION

A man who possesses common sense and the use of reason must not expect to learn from treatises or lectures on textual criticism anything that he could not, with leisure and industry, find out for himself. What the lectures and treatises can do for him is to save him time and trouble by presenting to him immediately considerations which would in any case occur to him sooner or later.

A. E. HOUSMAN

D URING the formative years of graduate education in the United States, it was frequently the policy of university language departments to require of their students as doctoral dissertations critical editions of early works, and indeed the preparation of a critical edition has always been universally recognized by academic departments in all languages and literatures as constituting, *ipso facto* and *par excellence*, the kind of "contribution to knowledge" required by graduate faculties.

Although in recent years bibliographical and editorial projects have steadily yielded to more obviously "literary" studies, the truth remains that the preparation of a critical edition, whether of an ancient or a modern author, whether from MSS[1] or printed texts, whether of a famous or of a neglected work, involves more kinds of literary problems and brings into play more kinds of literary ability than any other task. The editor is asked to demonstrate a mastery of some form of palaeography, of language, of descriptive bibliography,. of textual criticism, of literary history, of critical analysis, and of original critical judgment. He must learn to analyze and summarize the often complex theories of others, to find principles for the organization of apparently disparate materials, to indicate trends in scholarship, and to justify his deviations from the judgments of his predecessors. And he must everywhere demonstrate

3

that, to quote Housman again, he has a "head, not a pumpkin, on his shoulders, and brains, not pudding, in his head." [2]

Perhaps one reason for the near demise of critical editing, especially of texts written before the advent of printing, is that basic instruction is not always available to the novice. Graduate programs in Classics still offer full-scale courses in palaeography, epigraphy, and textual criticism, to be sure, but the usual "Bibliography and Methods" courses in other areas have often shrunk to one-credit library hunts. The capable graduate student, fresh from a mixed bag of undergraduate period and author courses, is thus seldom given the training necessary for editing, and, encouraged by the faculty toward critical studies, hardly considers the preparation of a critical edition, especially one for which the earliest texts are MSS.

For it is in this early period that the most instruction is needed and the least available. Difficult and treacherous as the editing of printed texts may be, it at least does not require the deciphering of a cramped Gothic book hand or the reconstruction by recension, mainly on the basis of hypothetical and (sometimes conveniently) lost texts, of a genealogical stemma leading toward, if never quite to, an author's original which probably never existed.

And fortunately the editor of printed texts in English does have the written experience of the masters to fall back upon. McKerrow's *Introduction*, [3] whatever the changing fashions, continues to supply a firm technical foundation. The essays of Greg and Bowers and Dearing illuminate not only particular problems, but general principles as well. There is even in print an up-to-date anthology of bibliographical writings. [4]

There are, however, no equivalent works for the editor of MSS in Middle English, and so the novice editor must turn to the classical manuals and to the great masters of classical scholarship. Granted that he discovers superb technicians (Maas for example) and that the impact of Housman's "Preface to Manilius I" is one of the catatonic experiences of one's intellectual life, the student of English still must deal with examples which are foreign to him and with specialized problems of transmission he probably will never encounter. What he needs is some orientation in the palaeography, the language, and the textual tradition of the MSS of his own national literature and

some practical advice as to how to proceed. This small volume attempts, however inadequately, those two tasks.

The chapters which follow are thus designed for those beginning editors who have had little or no prior training in palaeography, in the Middle English language, or in textual criticism and so must deal with simple theoretical models and with general principles. They do not, indeed could not, cover all of the myriad technicalities of any of the areas treated, though through the notes and the bibliography they do point the way toward more detailed studies. But however general they may be, these chapters are intended to be everywhere useful. For example, the examination of recension does not begin, as is usual, with an already constructed genealogical table which the author proceeds to explicate, but with a few lines (obviously hypothetical!) in a few MSS which form the basis for a collation by means of which is constructed in a rudimentary but highly orthodox fashion an elementary stemma.

In the same way, the exercises which accompany the section on emendation attempt to involve the reader, albeit at a very simple level, in the kinds of problems faced in dealing with actual texts. We have, by the way, here borrowed the excellent device used by James Willis in *Latin Textual Criticism*. "Fearing that here and there might be found readers," writes Professor Willis, "who, having failed to make independently a single emendation of Scaliger's, Bentley's, or Madvig's [the ME student might substitute Skeat, Gollancz, and Kane], would revenge themselves by declaring that all the emendations in question were wrong, I have devised some questions where the normal situation is reversed: that is to say, I have deliberately corrupted a sound text." [5]

This small volume will not reverse the present direction of graduate education. But it is hoped that it will provide an encouragement and a guide to those graduate students (and their teachers) who see the need for the continuation of the tradition of Bentley and Housman, Manly/Rickert and Kane, and who appreciate the value of the training involved. And that need is very real indeed. Great as is our debt to the nineteenth-century MS editors of the Early English Text Society, we need to revise their texts and to bring up to date their notes and introductions. Popular poems like *Sir Gawain and the*

Green Knight have been edited again and again, sometimes unfortunately so, but a number of works which have attracted a fair amount of critical comment in the past few years—*Ancrene Riwle*, *William of Palerne*, the Alexander Fragments—exist only in antiquated, hard-to-come-by editions.

This manual, it must be understood, will not provide the editor with an answer book, nor with a history, nor even with a clear-cut methodology. Indeed there are no firm answers or reliable methodologies to be had:

> . . . textual criticism is not a branch of mathematics, nor indeed an exact science at all. It deals with a matter not rigid and constant, like lines and numbers, but fluid and variable; namely the frailties and aberrations of the human mind, and of its insubordinate servants, the human fingers. It therefore is not susceptible of hard-and-fast rules. It would be much easier if it were; and that is why people try to pretend that it is, or at least behave as if they thought so. Of course you can have hard-and-fast rules if you like, but then you will have false rules, and they will lead you wrong; because their simplicity will render them inapplicable to problems which are not simple, but complicated by the play of personality. A textual critic engaged upon his business is not at all like Newton investigating the motions of the planets: he is much more like a dog hunting for fleas. If a dog hunted for fleas on mathematical principles, basing his researches on statistics of area and population, he would never catch a flea except by accident. They require to be treated as individuals; and every problem which presents itself to the textual critic must be regarded as possibly unique.[6]

This book will hopefully then provide the novice editor with a practical introduction to a genuinely important subject and with a basic guide, not as reliable as Virgil, but equally well-intentioned. Eventually Dante must advance beyond Virgil's guidance; but, on the other hand, Virgil did successfully rescue the poet from the Wood of Error and did lead him safely into the Earthly Paradise. But this is further into the metaphor than we had intended to go.

NOTES TO INTRODUCTION

1. MS(S) is not only the usual modern abbreviation of manuscript(s), but is used in place of the words themselves. See *The MLA Style Sheet*, 2nd ed. (New York, 1969), 28.

2. A. E. Housman, "The Application of Thought to Textual Criticism," *A. E. Housman: Selected Prose*, ed. John Carter (Cambridge, 1961), 150.

3. Ronald B. McKerrow, *An Introduction to Bibliography for Literary Students* (Oxford, 1927).

4. O. M. Brock, Jr. and Warner Barnes, eds., *Bibliographical and Textual Criticism* (Chicago, 1969).

5. James Willis, *Latin Textual Criticism* (Urbana, 1972), x.

6. Housman, "The Application of Thought to Textual Criticism," 132–33.

PALAEOGRAPHY

But even when palaeography is kept in her proper place, as handmaid, and not allowed to give herself the airs of mistress, she is apt to be overworked.

A. E. HOUSMAN

S INCE the editor faced with the MSS of a given work cannot rationally decide either upon their arrangement or upon which of them he will eventually settle as a copy-text, the basis of his edition, without first reading them carefully, he must master palaeography, the art of reading and interpreting ancient writings.

While a knowledge of the history of palaeography is certainly not necessary to the deciphering of medieval English texts, a short description of its scope and definitions of a few of its terms will help the student in reading the literature in the field, which is quite technical. The ensuing discussion is thus brief and oversimplified; the editor who needs amplification at any point is directed to more detailed authorities, particularly to Denholm-Young, who discusses at length those variant hands (such as the late Welsh Insulars) which this manual must perforce omit, to Johnson and Jenkinson, whose illustrations of all the individual scripts and characters are extremely helpful, and to Sir Maunde Thompson, whose statements of principles, albeit directed toward classical problems, are standard in the field.

In the widest possible sense of the term, palaeography includes all forms of writings in all times on all kinds of material—on stone, metal, and clay (epigraphy), coins (numismatics), seals (sphragistics), potsherds (ostraca), and walls (graffiti). In actual practice, however, palaeography is usually restricted to the study of hand-

9

writing, as distinct from engraving, on soft materials such as vellum, papyrus, or paper. Most definitions would include also the dating, placing, and description of MSS within the palaeographer's domain. And indeed, even when one restricts the term to the deciphering, dating, and placing of handwriting on soft materials, an incredible number of factors are involved in the total study—the form which the MS takes (roll, codex), the writing implements (style, reed, quill, ink), process of illumination, binding, particular circumstances of publication, provenance of the work, and, in fact, the whole history of its publication.

It is necessary also to separate "palaeography," which deals with all kinds of writings, from "diplomatic," which is the study of various aspects—form, authenticity, etc.—of charters, deeds, and like documents and from "bibliography," which we here rather arbitrarily restrict to the study of printed books.

These distinctions stem, of course, from the historical evolution of the uses of writing. The common letter form of both ancient epigraphy and palaeography is the "square Roman capital" (Fig. 1),[1] which in the hands of a master is, as is all subsequent writing, both

SQUARE ROMAN CAPITAL

VIRGIL.—FOURTH OR FIFTH CENTURY

(at venus ascanio placidam per mem[bra quietem] iamque ibat dicto parens et dona cu[pido]
inrigat' et fotum gremio dea tollit [in altos]   regia portabat tyriis' duce laetus [achate]
idaliae lucos' ubi mollis amaracu[s illum]   cum venit' aulaeis iam se regina s[uperbis]
floribus' et dulci adspirans comp[lectitur umbra] aurea composuit sponda' mediam[que locavit])

(Taken from E. M. Thompson, *Greek and Latin Palaeography*)

Figure 1

RUSTIC CAPITAL

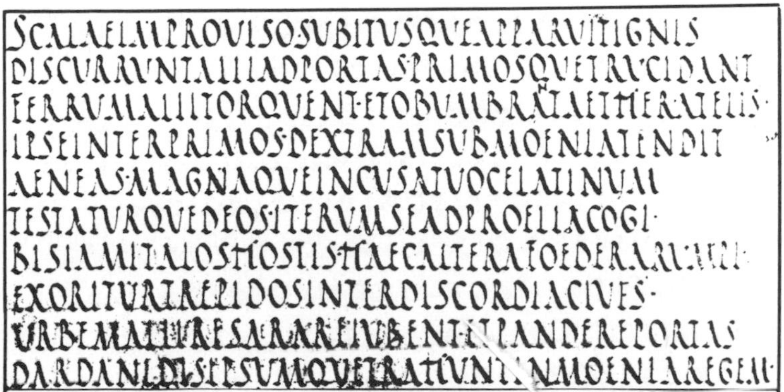

VIRGIL (Cod. Palat.)—FIFTH CENTURY
(Taken from E. M. Thompson)

Figure 2

an art medium and a vehicle for communication. The square Roman capital, however, being essentially a chiseller's form, was too wasteful of space and too time-consuming in production for efficient communication. So in the first century, with the appearance of soft writing material, the form yielded except for ceremonial and special uses (such as titles) to "rustic capitals," a less severe style made with a broad pen held obliquely (Fig. 2). In about the third century, these rustic majuscules[2] began to be rounded off with the aid of a semi-straight pen into "uncials," a more rounded cursive capital (Fig. 3). Some 200 years later appeared the "half-uncial," written with a perfectly straight pen and displaying an even more rounded majuscule mixed with minuscules in which parts of the letters (e.g. *g* and *h*) descended below or ascended above the square box of the majuscule (Fig. 4).

However, even during the centuries in which these beautifully conceived and wrought hands were used, there was developing simultaneously, though slowly at first, a form of writing more suitable for business, a more cursive script in which the pen was lifted from the page less often, the so-called "Roman cursive minuscule" (Fig. 5).

This parallel development, from square capitals to half-uncials

UNCIAL

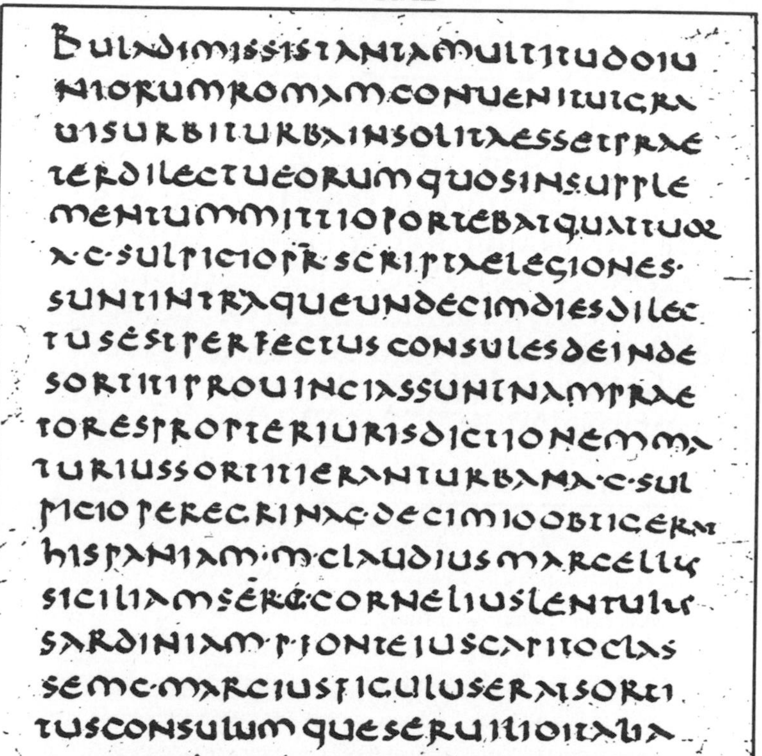
BULADIMISSISTANTAMULTITUDOIU
NIORUMROMAMCONUENITUTGRA
UISURBITURBAINSOLITAESSETPRAE
TERDILECTUEORUMQUOSINSUPPLE
MENTUMMITTIOPORTEBATQUATTUOR
A·C·SULPICIOPR·SCRIPTAELEGIONES·
SUNTINTRAQUEUNDECIMDIESDILEC
TUSESTPERFECTUSCONSULESDEINDE
SORTITIPROUINCIASSUNTNAMPRAE
TORESPROPTERIURISDICTIONEMMA
TURIUSSORTITIERANTURBANA·C·SUL
PICIOPEREGRINAC·DECIMIOOBTIGERAT
HISPANIAM·M·CLAUDIUSMARCELLUS
SICILIAMSER·CORNELIUSLENTULUS
SARDINIAM·P·FONTEIUSCAPITOCLAS
SEM·C·MARCIUSFIGULUSERATSORTI
TUSCONSULUMQUESERUILIOITALIA
C·MARCIOMACEDONIAOBUENITLA
TINISQUEACTISMARCIUSEXTEMPLO
ESTPROFECTUSCEPIONEDEINDERE
FERENTEADSENATUQUASEXNOUIS
LEGIONIBUSDUASLEGIONESSECUMIN
GALLIAMDUCERETDECREUEREPATRES
UTC·SULPICIUS·M·CLAUDIUSPR·EXHIS
QUASSCRIPSISSENTLEGIONIBUSQUAS
UIDERENTURCONSULIDARENTINDIG
NEPATIENTEPRAETORUM[illegible]
[illegible]
ADTRIBUNALPRAETORUM[illegible]

LIVY—FIFTH CENTURY
(Taken from E. M. Thompson)

Figure 3

HALF-UNCIAL

St. Augustine.—Sixth Century

(unt; Nemo enim vult esse freniticus˙ etiam | si videat frenetici vires˙ viribus sanorum es|se fortiores; praecipue igitur˙ doctrina sana | bonitatem propositi˙ et ornet et muniat; inde | est quippe quod catholicae feminae etiam |, saepius nubtae˙ Non solum univiris viduis˙ | sed et virginibus hereticorum˙ iusto iudicio | praeferuntur; multi sunt quidem de his tri|bus rebus˙ coniugii viduitatis˙ et virginitatis | quaestionum sinus · multae perplexitates˙ qui|bus disputando penetrandis vel dissolven|dis · et maiore cura opus est˙ et copiosiore ser|mone˙ ut vel in omnibus eis recte sapiamus˙)

(Taken from E. M. Thompson)

Figure 4

ROMAN CURSIVE MINUSCULE

Letter.—Fourth Century

(Cum in omnibus bonis benignitas tua sit praedita tum | etiam scholasticos et maxime qui a me cultore tuo hono|rificentiae tuae traduntur quod honeste respicere velit | non dubito domine praedicabilis quapropter theofanen | oriundum ex civitate hermupolitanorum provinciae | thebaidos qui ex suggestione domini mei fratris(nostri | [filippi usque ad officium] domini mei dyscoli vexationem)

(Taken from E. M. Thompson)

Figure 5

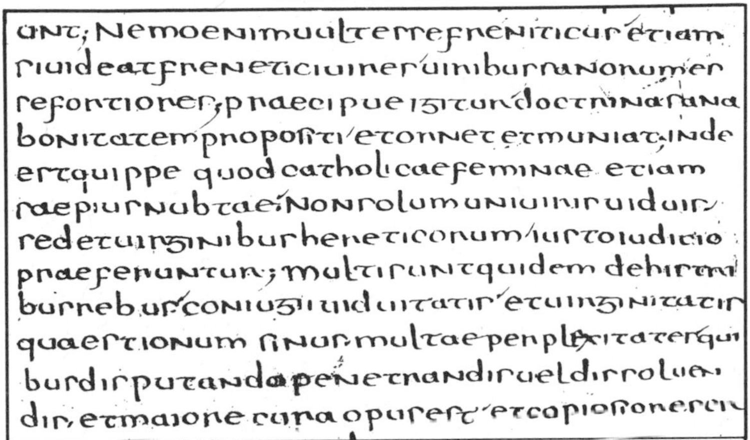

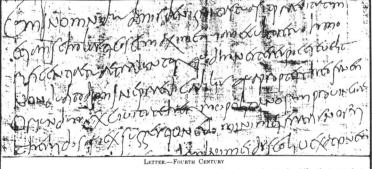

and from uncials to cursive minuscules, illustrates very well one of the great distinctions in the study of palaeography—the separation of the calligraphic "book" or "text" or "literary" hands from the more cursive "business" or "charter" or "court" hands. Their differences are due to the uses to which they are put: the values of a book hand used to produce a literary MS are clarity and beauty, while those of a court hand used to turn out legal and business documents are speed and ease of production. The various book hands are thus marked by even, regular, clearly-separated characters, the court hands by slurred, curved, cursive script. The two styles, of course, overlap; a trained scribe could presumably turn out whatever quality of work he was commissioned to do.

We are here, however, concerned primarily with the book hands of medieval England. While the semi-uncial script continued to be the principal book hand of Europe until the ninth century, from the sixth to the eighth century so-called national hands developed from various forms of reduced cursive minuscule, principally Merovingian, Visigothic, and Beneventan. The development of these national hands was made possible by the dissolution of the Roman imperium, and their reduced, cramped forms came about at least partly as an economy measure, since sheep and calf skins were expensive. However, the justly famed Anglo-Irish or insular hands, both rounded majuscule and pointed minuscule, brought to Lindesfarne from Iona by the Irish missionaries of the seventh century seem to be derived from half-uncial rather than cursive forms. The Lindesfarne Gospels (Fig. 6) are written in insular majuscule, which is actually a rounded half-uncial written obliquely with a narrow pen.

The various national hands, however, were in the main awkward and tedious and resulted in a great number of experimental scripts using local forms and abbreviations. The problem created by this diversity of hands was solved by the introduction of an extremely legible and aesthetically satisfying script from the continent, the "Caroline" or "Carolingian minuscule," which by the ninth century had become the dominant European book hand and in fact so remained for over 300 years (Fig. 7). Smaller than the majuscule scripts but much clearer than the national minuscules, the Caroline

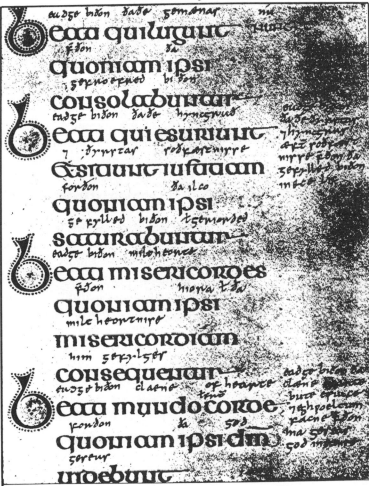

LINDISFARNE GOSPELS.—ABOUT A.D. 700

(Beati qui lugunt nunc | quoniam ipsi | consolabuntur | Beati qui esuriunt |
et sitiunt iustitiam | quoniam ipsi | satur..buntur | Beati misericordes | quo-
niam ipsi | misericordiam | consequentur | Beati mundo corde | quoniam ipsi
de*um* | videbunt ‖ *Gloss:* eadge biðon ða ðe gemænas nú | forðon ða | gefroe-
fred biðon | eadge biðon ða ðe hyncgrað | *and* ðyrstas soðfæstnisse | forðon
ða ilco | gefylled biðon *vel* geriorded | eadge biðon miltheorte | forðon hiora
vel ða | miltheortnise | him gefylges | eadge biðon claene of *vel* from hearte |
forðon ða god | geseas ‖ eadge biðon ða ðe ðyrstas *and* hyncgras æfter soð-
fæstnisse forðon ða gefylled biðon in ece lif. ‖ eadge biðon ða clæne hearte
bute esuice *and* eghwoelcum facne forðon hia geseas god in ecnise)

(Taken from E. M. Thompson)

Figure 6

hand featured from its inception certain characteristic letters—the cursive looped *g*, a reduced uncial *a*—but its greatest reform was in the exactness with which it was used. The letters in time became thinner, less "clubbed" or thickened, more upright, and as a consequence more uniformly legible.

The Caroline minuscule evidently reached England in the tenth century, where it existed side-by-side for a time with the two insular

CAROLINGIAN MINUSCULE

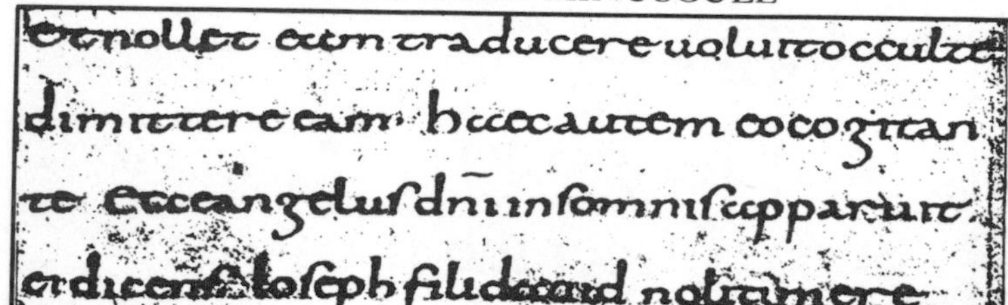

GOSPELS OF NEVERS.—ABOUT A.D. 840
(et nollet eam traducere voluit occulte | dimittere eam . Haec autem eo cogi-
tan|te ecce angelus domini in somnis apparuit | ei dicens . Ioseph fili david noli
timere | accipere mariam coniugem tuam . quod | enim ex ea nascetur de
spiritu sancto est . Pariet | autem filium et vocabis nomen eius iesum | Ipse
enim salvum faciet populum suum á pec|catis eorum . Hoc autem totum
factum est . | ut adimpleretur quod dictum est á domino | per prophetam
dicentem . Ecce virgo)
(Taken from E. M. Thompson)

Figure 7

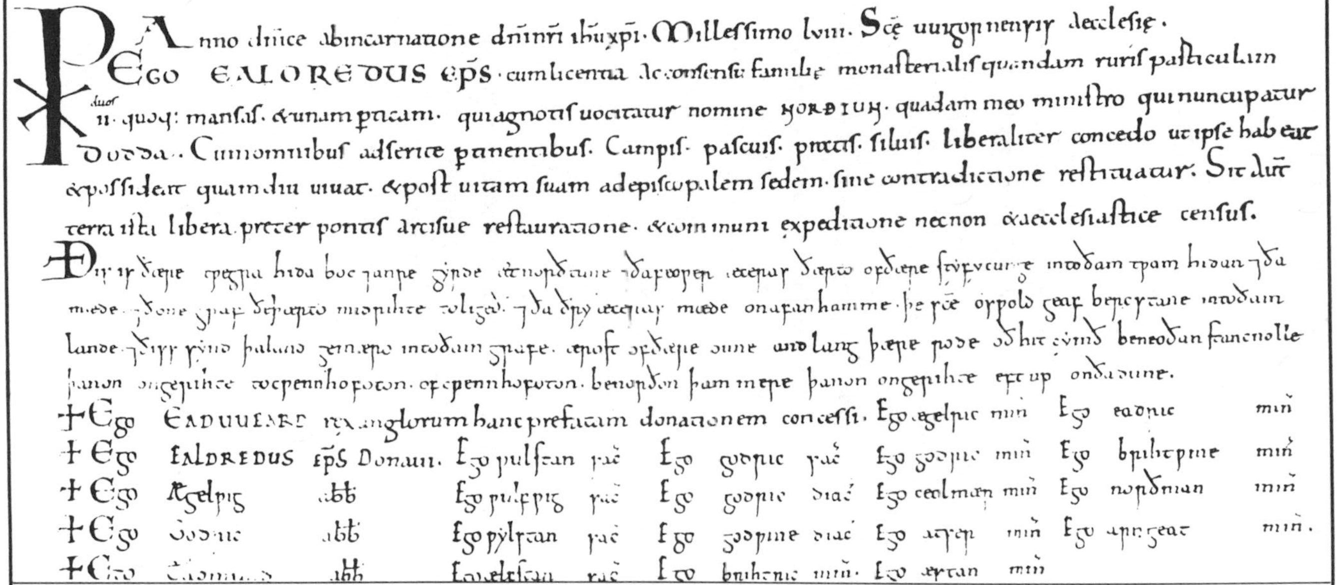

CAROLINGIAN AND INSULAR SCRIPTS

LATIN LAND GRANT—A.D. 1058

Figure 8

(Taken from N. Denholm-Young, *Handwriting in England and Wales*.)

GOTHIC MINUSCULE

hands. In time, the insular majuscule disappeared, but the distinctively pointed insular minuscule remained to form the basis for the court hands of the twelfth century and following. During the Old

TRANSCRIPTION

```
                god
and óft/kan mare þanc ðan ðe hím ȝíuet lesse
    eal hís peorkes 7 hís peies ís milce 7 rihtpisnesse
líte lác is gode leof . ðe cumeð of gode ipille
    7 eðlece muchel ȝíue ðenne ðe heorte is ille
heuene 7 eorðe he oue[r] sihð . his éȝen beoð spo brihte
    Sunne . mone . dei . 7 fur . bið þustre to ȝeanes his líhte
nis hī naht for hole . ni húd . spa michel bið his mihte
                     n
    nis hit na spá dur/e idón ᛫ né aspa þustre nihte
        hpet
hé pát/deð . 7 ðenchet . ealle quike pihte
    nis na hlauord spilc se ís crist . na king spílch ure drihtc
heouene 7 eorðe . 7 eal þet is . biloken in his hande
    he deð eal ꝥ his pille ís . á pétere and á lande
he makede fisces in ðe sé . 7 fuȝeles in ðe lufte
    he pít 7 pealdeð ealle ðing . 7 hé scop ealle ȝesceafte
he is ord abuten orde . 7 ende abuten ende
    hé ane is æure enelche stede . pende þer þu pende
he is buuen us 7 bi neoðen . bi foren 7 bi hinde
    þe ðc godes pille deð . eiðer he mei hím finde
elche rune hé ihurð . 7 he pat ealle dede
    he ðurh sihð ealches mannes ðanc . phet sceal us to rede
þeðe brekeð godes hése . 7 gultet spa ilome
    hpet scule pé seggen oðer don . æt ðe muchele dome
þa ða luueden unriht . 7 uuel líf ledde
    hpet scule hí segge oðer dón . ðer engles beoð of dredde
hpet scule pé béren bi foren . mid hpan scule pe cpeman
    pé þe næure gód ne duden . þe heuenliche démen
þer scule beon deofles spa uéle . ðe pulleð us for preȝen
```

POEMA MORALE—A.D. c1225

(Taken from C. E. Wright, *English Vernacular Hands.*)

Figure 9

English period, the native insular script, principally because it boasted the special characters thorn (þ), yogh (ȝ), and eth (ð), was the natural vehicle for Anglo-Saxon writings while the Caroline hand was reserved for Latin manuscripts; in fact, the two appear together in the royal charters of the tenth and eleventh centuries (Fig. 8).

GOTHIC MINUSCULE

The Caroline minuscule began to lose its European domination with the appearance toward the end of the eleventh century in France of what is called "Gothic minuscule," an angular rather than a rounded script, perpendicular and spiky, close and stiff, and in its later forms quite coarse. It is with the many different forms of this latter hand that the student of Middle English MSS must principally deal (Figs. 9–12). For while the liturgical forms of Gothic minuscule in most parts of Europe developed into an elegant perfection, in

TRANSCRIPTION

ꝥ mon seıs ıs sparepe uuel . Godd
hıt pıle for þı:ʹ ꝥ ho beo eaủ eadʹ
mod ⁊ pıð lah haldınge of hı
reseluē falle dun to þe eorðe leʹ
ste ho prude . Nu pe hurten
leue chıldre to þe feorðe dale .
ꝥ ı seıde schulde beō of feole fon
dīges . for þer beō uttre ⁊ ínre . ⁊
eıðer monı falde . Salue ıbıhet
to teachen to ȝeínes hā ⁊ boʹ
te . And hu þase haues ham
mcı Gederen of þıs dale conʹ
fort ⁊ froure to ȝaínes ham
alle . Þat ıch þurh þe lare of
þe halı gast mote halde forepʹ
ard:ʹ he hıt ȝeatı me þurh opʹ
re bones .
Ne pene nan of heh lıf ꝥ
ho ne beo ítēpted . Mare
beō þe gode ꝥ arn ıclūben
hehe ítēptet þē þe pake . And tat
ıs reısun . for se þe hul ıs herre of
halı lıf ⁊ of heh:ʹ spa þe feōdes
puffes . þe pínd of fondīges arn
strēgere þron . ⁊ mare . ȝıf aní
anker ıs ꝥ ne feles nane fon

dīges:ʹ spıðe drede ı ꝥ poínt . ꝥ ho
ḅẹọ beo oủ muchel ⁊ oủ spıðe ıfonʹ
det . for spa seın Greg' seıs . Tunc
maxıme ımpugnarıs c̄ te īpugʹ
narı nō sentıs . Sek mō haues
tpa estat spıðe dredfule . ꝥ an ís
hpē he ne feles napt hıs ahen secʹ
nesse . ⁊ forþı ne seches napt ne
leache . ne leachecraft . ne ne asʹ
kes na mō read . ⁊ asteorues ferʹ
lıche ear mō least pene . Þıs ıs te
anker ꝥ nat nopt hpat ıs fonʹ
dīge . To þeose spekes te engel ı þe
apocalıpse . Dıcıs quıa dıues sū
et nıīı egeo . et nescıs quıa mıser
es ⁊ paup ⁊ cec' . Þu seıs te nís ned
na medecíne . Ah þu art blínd
ıhertet . ní ne sest napt hu þu art
poure ⁊ naked of halínesse . ⁊
Gastlıche precche . Þat oðer dredʹ
ful estat ꝥ te seke haues:ʹ ıs al frāʹ
pard tıs . ꝥ ıs hpē he feles se muchʹ
el angoısse . ꝥ he ne maı þolıen ꝥ
mō hōdlen hıs sar . ní ꝥ mō hī hea
le þıs ıs sum anker ꝥ feles se

ANCRENE RIWLE—A.D. c1225

(Taken from C. E. Wright)

Figure 10

thirteenth-century England it became mixed with the cursive court hands when employed in writing vernacular literature. Denholm-Young notes that "as the Anglo-Saxon script broke up before the advance of court hand, writers of English did not turn to text (or book hand) as a substitute, but adopted a modified . . . form of the court hand in use for Latin or French documents." [3] The handwriting of most Middle English MSS is thus best described as a "slightly formal court hand written in a book-hand spirit," [4] which in its late

GOTHIC MINUSCULE

fourteenth-century and later forms was called by printers *lettre batarde* (Fig. 13).

The illustrations which accompany this text cannot hope to convey even a fragmentary notion of the immense variety in letter formation evidenced in the period. Likewise the chart of letter forms which follows (Figures 14–16) is meant only as a general guide

Ich þas ín one suṁe dale .
In one suþe [sic MS.] di3ele hale .
Iherde ich holde grete tale .
An hule and one ni3tíngale .
Þat plaıt þas stıf ⁊ starc ⁊ strõg .
Sum þıle softe ⁊ lud among .
An asþer a3en oþer sval .
⁊ let þat wole mod ut al .
⁊ eıþer seıde of oþeres custe .
þat alçre þorste þat hı þuste .
⁊ hure ⁊ hure of oþere songe
Hı holde plaıdıng suþe stronge .
e ni3tıngale bıgon þe speche .
In one hurne of one broche .
⁊ sat upone vaıre bo3e .
þar þere abute blosme ino3e .
In ore þaste þıcke hegge .
I meínd mıd spııe ⁊ grene segge
Ho þas þe gladur uor þe rıse .
⁊ song auele cunne þíse .
Het þu3te þe dreím þat he þere .
Of harpe ⁊ pıpe þan he nere .
Bet þu3te þat he þere ıshote .
Of harpe ⁊ pıpe þan of þrote .
þ o stod on old stoc þarbısıde .
þar þo vle song hıre tíde .
⁊ þas mıd íuí albıgroþe .
Hıt þas þare hule eardıngstoþe .
þ e ni3tıngale hı ıse3 .
⁊ hı bıhold ⁊ ouerse3 .
⁊ þu3te þel wl of þare hule .
For me hı halt lodlıch ⁊ fule .
vn þı3t ho sede a þeı þu flo .
Me ıs þe wrs þat ıch þe so .

Iþıs for þıne wle lete .
þel oftích mıne song forlete .
Mın horte atflıþ ⁊ falt mı tonge
þonne þu art to me ıþrunge .
Me luste bet speten þane sınge .
Of þıne fule 3o3elínge .
os hule abod fort hıt þas [sic MS.] eve .
Ho ne mı3te no leng bıleue .
vor híre horte þas so gret .
þat þelne3 hıre fnast at schet .
⁊ þarp a þord þar aft' longe .
Hu þíncþe nu bı míne songe .
þest þu þat ıch ne cunne sínge .
þe3 ıch ne cunne of þrıtelınge [sic MS.] .
Ilome þu dest me'g'me
⁊ seıst me boþe tone ⁊ schaṁe .
3ıf ıch þe holde on mıne note .
So hıt bıtıde þat ıch mote .
⁊ þu þere vt of þíne rıse .
þu sholdest sínge an oþer þ[ı]se .
e ni3tıngale 3af answare .
3ıf ıch me lokı þıt þe bare .
⁊ me schılde þıt þe blete
Ne reche ıch no3t of þíne þrete .
3ıf ıch me holde ın mıne hegge .
Ne recche ıch neû þhat þu segge .
Ich þot þat þu art un mılde .
wıþ hom þat ne mu3e frõ se schılde .
⁊ þu tukest wroþe ⁊ vuele .
whar þu mí3t over smale fu3ele .
vorþı þu art loþ al fuel kunne .
⁊ alle ho þe dríueþ honne .
⁊ þe bı schrícheþ ⁊ bıgredet .
⁊ wel nareþe þe bıledet .

THE OWL AND THE NIGHTINGALE—A.D. c1250.

(Taken from C. E. Wright)

Figure 11

(though it does include most major forms); the reader is referred again to Johnson and Jenkinson for variant forms, for in the end, the editor must learn the art of palaeography not from a manual, but from a particular manuscript (or a facsimile of one) written by a particular scribe.

Just as an individual scribe comes to develop his own peculiarities in handwriting, so will he also use symbols and abbreviations which differ from the common stock. The standard abbreviations, however, derive for the most part from Latin MSS where they provide a

GOTHIC MINUSCULE

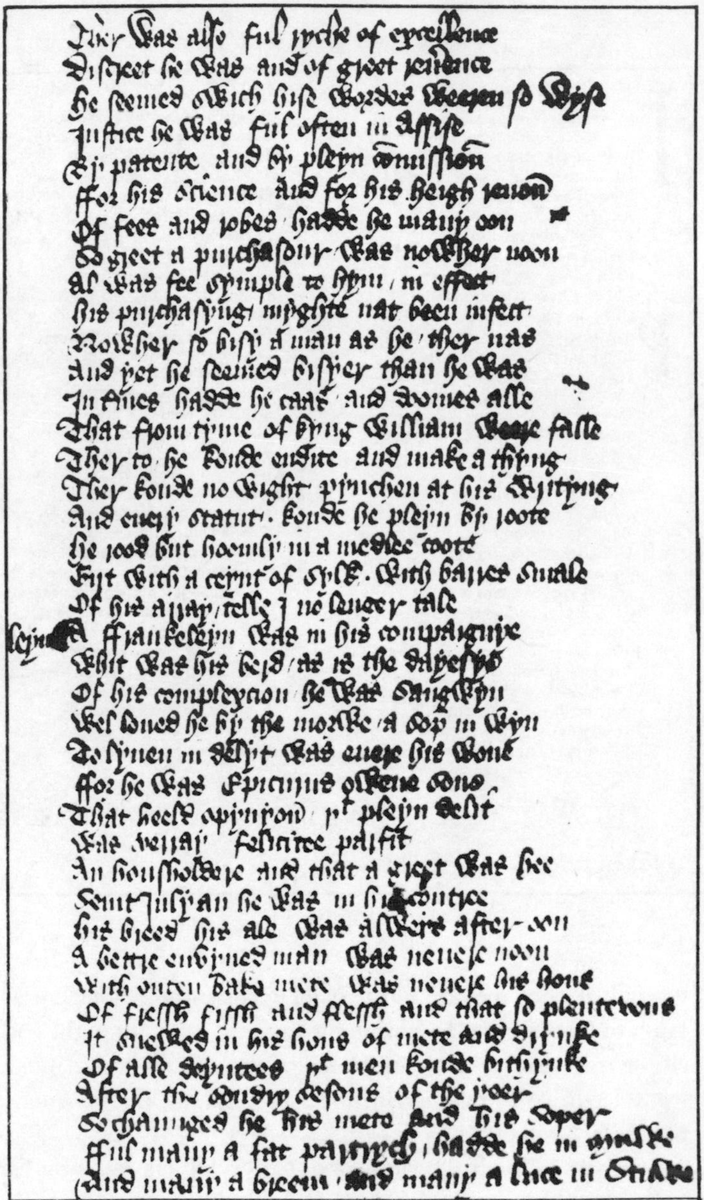

THE CANTERBURY TALES—A.D. c1410

Figure 12

means of economy, a labor-saving device, and perhaps, with contractions, a means of avoiding the copying out of the *nomina sacra*. In general, palaeographers divide abbreviations into four classes:

1. Suspensions: the omission of final letters, designated either by a final dot (R. = Rex) or by a superior horizontal line or other marking over the last letter (regē=regem).

2. Contractions: the omission of medial letters, designated by a horizontal line above the omission (n̄r, n̄o, n̄m, n̄rm=noster).

3. Superior letters: omission of either final or medial letters, designated by raised characters (ṁ=mihi, qᵘm=quam).

4. Special signs: more or less arbitrary symbols originating from a variety of sources. Among the most common are:[5]

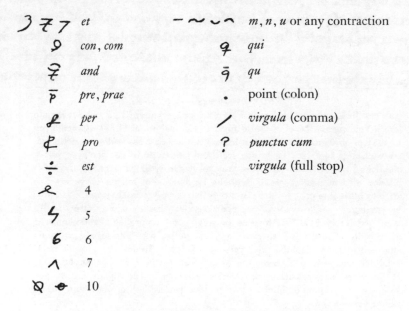

ꝫ ⁊ �4	*et*	‒ ∼ ⌣ ⌢	*m, n, u* or any contraction
ꝯ	*con, com*	ꝗ	*qui*
⁊	*and*	q̄	*qu*
p̄	*pre, prae*	.	point (colon)
ꝑ	*per*	/	*virgula* (comma)
ꝓ	*pro*	⸮	*punctus cum*
÷	*est*		*virgula* (full stop)
ꝝ	4		
ꝗ	5		
6	6		
⋀	7		
ꝗ ⊕	10		

Mention should be made of the dating and arranging of MSS from palaeographical evidence if for no other reason than to inspire caution.[6] Jenkinson notes that "court hand documents can generally be read with certainty, but only in the light of their meaning, and that they can nearly always be dated with accuracy, but not by their

LETTRE BATARDE

AYENBITE OF INWYT.—A.D. 1340

(ine þise live. Ac þise bȳeþ ȳefþes ariȝt wȳþoute wȳþnȳmȳnge / and wȳþou|te
lere. Vor huanne þe oþre ssolle faȳli / þise ssolle ous bleve. Þanne bȳeþ
hi zuo | propreliche oure ∶ þet we his ne moȝe naȝt lȳese wȳlle we nolle we.
ase we | moȝe ꝼe oþre. Þe þridde scele and þe heȝeste is. vor þer bȳeþ ȳefþes
clenliche | be love. and þou wost wel þet ȳefþe lȳest þane name of ȳefþe ∶
huanne hit | ne is naȝt ȳȳeve clenliche be love. Vor huanne þe ȳevere heþ
ziȝꝼe to his oȝe|ne prov ∶ þet ne is no ȳefþe ∶ ac raþre is chapvare. Huanne
he ȳzȳȝþ guod|nesse ondervonge / oꝼe'r' service / þet ne is no ȳefþe / ac hit
is raþre dette ȳȳol|de. Ac huanne þe ȳefþe comþ proprelich'e' and chenliche
of þe welle of love wiþ|oute prov. wȳþoute ȳefþe. wȳ'þ'oute drede. wȳþoute
enie dette ∶ þanne is hit | ariȝt ȳcleped / ȳefꝼe. Huerof þe filosofe zaȳþ.
þet ȳefþe / is ȳevȳnge ∶ wȳþ|oute aȳenȳefþe. þet is wȳoute onderstondinge
of aȳenȳefþe. ac wȳþ|oute more ∶ vor to zeche love. Ine zuȳche manere god
ȳefþ ous his ȳefþes | clenliche / vor þe love þet he heþ to ous / and vor to
gaderi oure herten.)

(Taken from E. M. Thompson)

Figure 13

	MAJUSCULES		MINUSCULES	
A	1202	1379	1256	1292
	1229		1272	1381
B	1302	1371	1233	1330
	1307	1379	1272	1488
C	1272		1272	1360
	1391		1350	
D	1225	1350	1307	
	1328	1371	1335	
E	1229		1302	1417
	1371		1335	
F	1147		1301	
	1379		1391	
G	1202		1270	1392
	1328		1328	

Figure 14

H	1265		1256	1390	
	1340		1360		
I J	1350		1338	1360	
	1350		1360	1368	
K	1229		1315		
			1379		
L	1292		1315	1371	
	1307		1360		
M N	1233	1350	1167	1381	
	1272	1360	1288	1392	
O	1381		1330		
P	1340		1350		
			1371		
Q	1256		1368		
	1338		1399		

Figure 15

R	1335		1256	1330
	1338		1330	
S	1340		1319	1390
	1379		1381	
T	1204		1381	
	1301		1390	
U V	1390		1288	
	1391		1392	
W	1315			
	1379			
X			1368	
Y			1379	
			1436–1450	
Z	1229			
	1335			

Figure 16

handwriting," [7] to which Denholm-Young adds that this principle is doubly true with book hands. Nevertheless, certain broad changes may be observed, and the student's first task should be to compare his specimen with textbook MSS already dated in order to form a general opinion of the hand in terms of its period and the region of its production. Having reached at least a tentative notion of the circumstances of composition, he may then attempt to apply what few generalizations can be made concerning the individual characters in order to reach a more precise dating (for example, that *ff* appears for F as early as 1240 and that final *f* yields to *s* only in the late thirteenth century). Johnson and Jenkinson's dated examples are of great value here.

After attempting to date and place the MS, the student should go on to prepare for his own future use a full bibliographical description of his MSS, of which Denholm-Young provides a fine model:

> State at the outset the general contents of the manuscript, specifying any portion which may be of outstanding importance. Then give the language, date, and (if ascertainable) provenance, and place where the manuscript was written. Say whether it is on paper (watermarks to be noticed) or parchment. Give the size of the writing-block (page or column), and page; the ruling if prior to *c.* A.D. 1200 (i.e. if it is by dry-point rather than lead plummet); number of lines to page or column; number of leaves (apparent and real); collation, if possible; contemporary quire signatures and foliation or pagination; binding (material, style, date, provenance, traces of fastenings or chaining); history (former owners, arms, book-plates, genealogical notes, notes of sales and prices); notes of *peciae*.
>
> Note also definite changes of hand; the *incipit* (of prologue, text, and gloss, with *secundo folio incipit*) and *explicit* (of text and colophon). [8]

With such a description in hand, he is ready to edit, or at any rate almost ready.

NOTES TO PALAEOGRAPHY

1. In the figures which accompany the text several examples are left untranscribed as exercises for the student.

2. The palaeographer's term for large letters, either capitals or uncials, the small letters being minuscules.

3. N. Denholm-Young, *Handwriting in England and Wales* (Cardiff, 1964), 36. C. E. Wright's *English Vernacular Hands from the Twelfth to the Fifteenth Centuries* (Oxford, 1960) contains a number of nicely reproduced MS pages with transcriptions.

4. Denholm-Young, *Handwriting in England and Wales*, 36.

5. Denholm-Young, in *Handwriting in England and Wales* 64–70, and Johnson and Jenkinson, in *English Court Hand: A.D. 1066 to 1500*, 59–67, give lengthy lists.

6. Classical scholars have an easier time of establishing the relative chronology of their MSS than do medievalists, since the MSS of a given classical work generally extend over centuries and hence exhibit wider differences in palaeography than do manuscripts of a medieval work produced within a few years.

7. Denholm-Young, *Handwriting in England and Wales*, 81. This remark was made apropos of a demonstration by Jenkinson that a dozen documents which could have been dated as far as a century apart were actually written during the same year.

8. Denholm-Young, *Handwriting in England and Wales*, 84.

MIDDLE ENGLISH

*Among their pupils are several who comprehend neither Latin nor
any other language and whom nature has prodigally endowed at
birth with . . . hebetude of intellect.*

A. E. HOUSMAN

JUST as a knowledge of the basic facts of paleography will help
the novice editor to approach his task if not with expertise then at
least with some small measure of confidence, so will some
acquaintance with the standard forms of Middle English (provided
such exist!) alert him to the possibilities of scribal error. It should be
reiterated that in the realms neither of palaeography nor of language
will this manual suffice the professional editor, but the beginner can
at least use it to apply for citizenship in those countries, if not to
qualify for office therein.

The term "Middle English" is used to designate that period of the
language extending from the Norman invasion of 1066 to approxi-
mately 1500, an arbitrary date. The most notable effect of Norman
French upon Anglo-Saxon was on its word stock. In the two centuries subsequent to the invasion, during which England was essentially bilingual, the morphology of the root tongue (now a peasant
language) was simplified, and English began to emerge an analytic
rather than a synthetic language. More specifically, the Middle
English period was marked by a number of changes in vowel pronunciation, particularly in the merging and levelling of unstressed
vowels, which in turn caused both a drastic reduction in the number
of inflected forms in all parts of speech and the loss of grammatical
gender.

During the Middle English period, the dialect of London, essentially East Midland, became a standard for the rest of the country. London was, after all, the hub of trade and shipping, the seat of court and government, and the country's cultural center. The western nobleman or merchant, however great his distaste for the frivolities of Richard ii's court, had to speak either French or Londonese or both to conduct his affairs in the capital. It is this standardization of East Midland that makes Chaucer easier for us to read than Langland or the *Pearl*-poet. It is not, of course, strictly true that Chaucer's popularity established East Midland as the standard dialect, but the fact that he wrote in what was becoming the standard dialect does give the modern reader readier access to him than to his provincial contemporaries.

It is thus the purpose of this chapter to provide the student with a synopsis of the basic written forms of Chaucer's dialect, noting only incidentally varying dialectal or exceptional forms or systems (e.g. the so-called minor declensions). Its ultimate aim is not to supply the student with anything resembling a complete Middle English grammar, but simply to alert him to scribal, or even authorial, idiosyncrasies which may indicate the presence of significant variations in mss.[1] Changes in the spoken language are not discussed since the phonology of a language affects the reading of texts only in those instances where it influences the choice of a rhyming word.

I. The Noun

Middle English (me) nouns have singular and plural numbers; masculine, feminine, and neuter genders; and four cases—nominative, accusative, genitive, and dative. Their inflections are largely dependent upon their Old English (oe) forms.

In me, as in oe, nouns are divided into two classes, nouns which originally ended in a vowel (the strong declensions) and those which ended in *n* (the weak declensions).

A. Strong Masculine Nouns

To this declension belong the oe masculine *a*, *ja*, and *wa* stems,

the OE masculine *i* stems, and the OE masculine *u* stems. Sample
paradigms are as follows:

		OE	ME	CE	ME
Sing. Nom.	Acc.	*stān*	*stōn*	*engel*	*engel*
	Gen.	*stānes*	*stōnes*	*engles*	*engles*
	Dat.	*stāne*	*stŏn (e)*	*engle*	*engle*
Plural Nom.	Acc.	*stānas*	*stōnes*	*englas*	*engles*
	Gen.	*stāna*	*stōnes*	*engla*	*engles*
	Dat.	*stānum*	*stōnes*	*englum*	*engles*
Sing. Nom.	Acc.	*ende*	*ende*	*sunu*	*sone*
	Gen.	*endes*	*endes*	*suna*	*sones*
	Dat.	*ende*	*ende*	*sunu*	*sone*
Plural Nom.	Acc.	*endas*	*endes*	*suna*	*sones*
	Gen.	*enda*	*endes*	*suna*	*sones*
	Dat.	*endum*	*endes*	*sunum*	*sones*

A large number of nouns are declined like *stōn*, among them *arm*,
bōt, *cōmb*, *craft*, *dew*, *dōm*, *feld*, *fisch*, *gest*, *hōm*, *hound*, *king*, *schaft*, *snow*,
stol, *storm*, *swan*, and *wind*.

Nouns ending in *el*, *en*, *er*, such as *appel*, *crādel*, *girdel*, *hunger*,
punter, and *sadel*, are declined like *engel*.

B. Strong Neuter Nouns

To this declension belong the OE neuter *a*, *ja*, and *wa* stems and
the OE neuter *i* stems. These stems were inflected in OE exactly like
the corresponding masculines except that the nominative and accusative plurals ended either in *u* or had no endings, while the
masculine stems ended in *as*, which became *es* in ME.

These strong neuter nouns in ME thus formed their plurals by
adding *es* when the stem ended in a consonant *(bak, barn, bord, horn,
nest, ·schip)*, *s* when the stem ended in a vowel *(dāle, gāte, hōle, knē,
spēre, stēle, trē)*, or by remaining uninflected when denoting time,
weights, measures, or items viewed collectively *(dēr, folk, nēt, schēp,
swīn)*.

C. Strong Feminine Nouns

To this declension belong the OE *ō*, *jō*, and *wō* stems; the OE

feminine *i* stems; and the OE feminine *u* stems. Sample paradigms are as follows:

	OE	ME	OE	ME	OE	ME
Sing.						
Nom.	*talu*	*tāle*	*hwīl*	*whīle*	*cwēn*	*quēne*
Acc.	*tale*	*tāle*	*hwīle*	*whīle*	*cwēn*	*quēne*
Gen.	*tale*	*tāle(s)*	*hwīle*	*whīle(s)*	*cwēne*	*quēne(s)*
Dat.	*tale*	*tāle*	*hwīle*	*whīle*	*cwēne*	*quēne*
Plural						
Nom.	*tala, e*	*tāles*	*hwīla, e*	*whīles*	*cwēne, a*	*quēnes*
Acc.						
Gen.	*tala, ena*	*tāles*	*hwīla, ena*	*whīles*	*cwēna*	*quēnes*
Dat.	*talum*	*tāles*	*hwīlum*	*whīles*	*cwēnum*	*quēnes*

	OE	ME
Sing.		
Nom.	*hand*	*hand*
Acc.		
Gen.	*handa*	*hande(s)*
Dat.	*handa*	*hand(e)*
Plural		
Nom.	*handa*	*handes*
Acc.		
Gen.	*handa*	*handes*
Dat.	*handum*	*handes*

Among the words declined like *tāle* are *cāre, lengþe, nōse, schāde, schame,* and *wrāke;* like *while, blisse, brigge, cribbe, egge, fetere, glōve, helle, lōre, nēdle, sorwe, sould,* and *stowe;* like *quene, benche, brīde, dēde, hīve, spēde,* and *tide;* like *hand, blessing, ēvening, flor, lerning,* and *miʒt.*

D. The Weak or *N* Declension Nouns

This declension contained in OE masculine, feminine, and neuter nouns. Its typical endings are:

	OE	ME
Sing. Nom.	*a, e*	*e*
Acc. Gen. Dat.	*an*	*en*
Plural Nom. Acc.	*an*	*en*
Gen.	*ena*	*ene*
Dat.	*um*	*en*

Examples of nouns which belong to this declension in ME are *āpe*, *asche*, *asse*, *bēre*, *bukke*, *chirche*, *dogge*, *fōle*, *hāre*, *herte*, *lippe*, *mōne*, *nāme*, *oxe*, *pipe*, *sterre*, *widewe*, and *wolle*.

II. The Pronoun

The personal pronoun in ME takes the following forms:

SINGULAR

First Person		Second Person		Third Person	
Nom.	*I, ich(ik)*	*thou*	*he(e)*	*she*	*hit, hyt*
Gen.	*my, myn*	*thy, thyn*	*his*	*hir(e), her*	*his*
Dat.	*me*	*thee*	*him*	*hir(e), her(e)*	*him*
Acc.	*me*	*thee*	*him*	*hir(e), her(e)*	*hit, hyt*

PLURAL

Nom.	*we*	*ye*	*they*
Gen.	*oure*	*youre*	*hir(e), her(e)*
Dat.	*us*	*yow, you*	*hem*
Acc.	*us*	*yow, you*	*hem*

The reflexive pronouns are *myself*, *myselven*, *thyself*, and *thyselven*. The demonstrative prounouns take the following forms:

Sing.	*this*	*that*
Pl.	*this(e), these*	*tho(o)*

The indefinite pronoun, *al*, takes the forms:

Nom. Sing.	*al*
Nom. Pl.	*alle*
Gen. Pl.	*aller (alder)*

III. The Adjective

Although the distinction between strong and weak adjectives had become blurred by Chaucer's time, some separation was still observed and can be found in the monosyllabic adjectives ending in consonants. When the adjective in OE ended in a vowel, no distinction was made in ME, but in general the weak or definite form was used when the adjective was preceded by the definite article or a

demonstrative or possessive pronoun, when it was used as a noun, when it modified a noun in the vocative, or when it modified a proper noun.

The two systems may be seen in *yong* and *swete*:

	Strong	Weak
Sing.	*yong*	*yonge*
Pl.	*yonge*	*yonge*
Sing.	*swete*	*swete*
Pl.	*swete*	*swete*

Adjectives of more than one syllable (e.g. *litel*, *blisful*) are generally uninflected.

The regular suffixes for the comparison of adjectives are those of Modern English, *er* and *est*, though a number of adjectives are irregularly compared:

> *good, bettre, best*
> *bad, badder* (or *werse*), *werste*
> *muchel, more* (or *mo*), *most*
> *lytel, lasse, leeste*

IV. The Adverb

The regular endings of ME adverbs are *e* and *ly* or *liche* (*brighte*, *royalliche*, *royally*, *smerte*), though there are a few adverbs in *es* or *en* which correspond to those in OE ending in *es* or *an* (*aboven*, *abuten*, *hennes*, *ones*, *twyes*).

V. The Verb

ME verbs can be separated into weak and strong conjugations. Strong verbs, sometimes called irregular, form their preterites by changing the root vowel and weak verbs by adding an ending (*de* or *te*). The principal parts of the strong verbs are generally those of modern English; the inflectional endings are shown in the following tables. *N* may always be dropped in the verbal ending *en*, and the prefix *y* may or may not be used with participles.

Present tense (strong and weak)

Indicative		Subjunctive	
Singular 1.	*singe*	Singular	*singe*
2.	*singest*	Plural	*singe (n)*
3.	*singeth*		
Plural	*singe(n)*		

A number of verbs have contracted forms in the second and third singular, such as *lixt (liest)*, *bit (biddeth)*, and *set (setteth)*.

Preterite Indicative
Strong

Singular 1.	*song, sang*
2.	*song(e)*
3.	*song, sang*
Plural	*songe(n)*

Weak

Singular 1.	*wende*	*lovede*
2.	*wendest*	*lovedest*
3.	*wende*	*lovede*
Plural	*wende(n)*	*lovede(n)*

The preterite subjunctive, like the present, ends in *e* in the singular and *e(n)* in the plural.

Imperative
Strong

Singular	*sing*
Plural	*singeth, -e*

Weak

Singular	*loke*	*her*
Plural	*loketh, -e*	*hereth, -e*

The infinitive ending is *en* or *e* in strong and weak verbs alike.
The present active participle of all verbs ends in *ing* or *inge*, e.g. *singing(e)*, *loving(e)*; the preterite passive participle of strong verbs

ends in *e(n)*, of weak verbs in *d* or *t*. The prefix *y* appears frequently in both strong and weak verbs.

In a small class of verbs an old strong preterite came to be used as a present tense, and a new weak preterite was formed to express past time. Such verbs are known as preterite–present verbs. For example:

	Present			Preterite	
Singular	1. *shal*		Singular	1. *sholde*	
	2. *shalt*			2. *sholdest*	
	3. *shal*			3. *sholde*	
Plural	*shull (en)*, *shal*		Plural	*sholde(n)*	

Other preterite–present verbs are *can* (pret. *kouthe*, *koude*); *dar* (pret. *dorste*); *may* (pret. *mighte*); *most* (pret. *moste*); *owe* (pret. *oughte*); and *woot* (pret. *wiste*).

A very few verbs show exceptional irregularities:

Goon (pret. *yede* and *wente*)
Doon (pret. *dide*)
Been

	Present Indicative	
Singular	1. *am*	
	2. *art*	
	3. *is*	
Plural	*are*, *arn*, *be(n)*	

	Present Subjunctive
Singular	*be*
Plural	*bes*

	Preterite Indicative	
Singular	1. *was*	
	2. *were*	
	3. *was*	
Plural	*were (n)*	

	Preterite Subjunctive
Singular	*were*
Plural	*were (n)*

	Imperative
Singular	*be*
Plural	*beeth*

The syntax of Middle English differs very little from that of the

present language, though the constructions of the older period are more flexible. Sudden changes of tense are usual; juxtaposition of sentence elements without connectives occurs; changes in strict grammatical construction are common; subjects and predicates do not always agree; pronouns often lack antecedents. However, since any of the good handbooks can supply long lists of such variant syntactical usages and forms as the double negative, the omission of the preposition, and the impersonal constructions and of the usual idioms of the period, it seems pointless to construct a partial list here. The editor is enjoined, however, to *note carefully* any apparent grammatical or syntactical idiosyncracies of his author and/or scribe, whether personal or dialectal, *item by item* as he encounters them in the hope that they may eventually resolve themselves into a pattern. Orthographic variations are seldom critical except as they may reflect pronunciation and hence rhyme; neither authors nor scribes had any great respect for spelling as such.

The novice editor needs also some rudimentary knowledge of Middle English versification. In general two systems were followed, though they frequently seem to merge and influence one another.

The "London poets," principally Chaucer, used the continental syllabic forms in which, as in almost all English post-Renaissance poetry, each line consisted of a pre-determined number of syllables (e.g. ten in pentameter) arranged according to a pattern of stressed and unstressed vowels (e.g. iambic). What makes Middle English verse of this kind difficult to read is the presence of a great many final *e*'s which apparently may or may not have been pronounced according both to their position in the line and their relation to the rhythm. The most widely accepted view would seem to be that final *e*'s are ordinarily pronounced in verse and are more often than not necessary for the rhythm. They are almost always pronounced when rhymed, and Chaucer avoided rhyming words ending in *e* with words not normally having that ending. But within the line final *e* is regularly elided before initial vowels and mute *h*'s. Apparently, before initial consonants *e* was ordinarily, though not universally, sounded.

The London poetry of the period, especially that of Chaucer, has great flexibility and freedom. It frequently shifts the position of the

caesura and often substitutes one kind of foot for another. It may even omit an initial syllable to form a "headless line" or add a light syllable to a line. In the hands of a master like Chaucer, the possibilities for rhythmic variation are well-nigh infinite.

The other kind of verse written in Middle English derives from another tradition, from native Anglo-Saxon rather than European stock. In the middle years of the fourteenth century, there appeared in the north and west of England a revival of the kind of alliterative, heroic poetry composed by the *scops* of pre-invasion Britain. The most famous poets of this Alliterative Revival are the so-called *Pearl-* or *Gawain*-poet and William Langland, author of *Piers Plowman*.

The verse of the Alliterative School inherits from its Anglo-Saxon ancestry the use of the unrhymed alliterative accentual line. The prevalence of this verse form, which Old English poetry shares with that of other Germanic languages, derives from two conditions, one linguistic—the tendency in all Germanic languages to place the major stress upon the initial syllable of the root word—the other literary—the comparative ease of oral composition in accentual, as opposed to syllabic, lines. Taken together these two factors result in the heaviest metrical accents falling upon the initial syllables of words and hence in the use of alliteration (which is simply heavily stressed, initial-syllable rhyme) as the natural poetic embellishment of primitive Germanic verse.

While there are variations in the alliterative line as it is used by Old and Middle English poets, the typical line generally consists of two half-lines or verses, each containing two major stresses (generally called lifts), rhetorically separated by a sharp caesura, but metrically joined by the alliterative pattern of the line, which is usually established by its third lift. Poets did indeed seek, and find, means of varying this essential pattern. The arguments and counterarguments of such modern analysts as Sievers, Leonard, Pope, and Bliss bear witness to the enormous subtleties of timing and accent that were possible. But the basic line itself was the metrical foundation of alliterative verse and is always discernible.

The prevailing use of the half-line as rhetorical unit serves to unify the whole corpus of alliterative poetry, since this habit of composition results in the "cumulative method of description, the piling up

of phrases, usually a half-line in length and often similar in construction" [2] which is distinctive of Old English poetry. It is clear also that Alliterative Revival poetry utilizes a special poetic vocabulary and a large stock of ready-made formulae, "stylized syntactically related collocations of words in regular rhythmic patterns," [3] each usually a half-line in length. The use of such formulae stems, as does the use of the accentual line, from the oral composition of the earliest poetry; a trained poet called upon to compose extempore could find in his stock of formulae an appropriate metrical phrase which could, by the simple substitution of noun or adjective, be made to fit both the occasion and the line. The better the poet the greater the originality and subtlety that could be employed, especially in written verse.

But the two systems frequently merge. Hence alliterative and accentual characteristics occasionally occur in Chaucer and rhyme in West Country poetry. Nevertheless, the editor may be able at times to determine a correct reading on the basis of a rhyme or an alliterative pattern. It is interesting to note that as one's knowledge of Middle English increases, one's willingness to generalize diminishes. While older editors frequently placed the origin of a given MS within a few miles on the basis of language, many modern editors are often reluctant to identify positively even a specific dialect but with, as Hotspur says, "proviso and exception."

But then with an editor, everything is but with proviso and exception.

NOTES TO MIDDLE ENGLISH

1. The student wishing detailed information should consult the standard grammars, most conveniently Karl Brunner, *An Outline of Middle English Grammar* (Cambridge, Mass., 1963), Fernand Mosse, *A Handbook of Middle English* (Baltimore, 1952), and Joseph and Elizabeth Wright, *An Elementary Middle English Grammar* (London, 1923).
2. Dorothy Everett, *Essays on Middle English Literature* (Oxford, 1955), 23.
3. Stanley B. Greenfield, *A Critical History of Old English Literature* (New York, 1965), 74.

TEXTUAL CRITICISM

Textual criticism is a science, and since it comprises recension and
emendation, it is also an art.
A. E. HOUSMAN

MANUSCRIPTS, like books, may be classified in any number
of ways, by date or place or scribal hand or subject matter,
depending on the ends or interests of the classifier. It is always a
shock to the American scholar, who is essentially a shelf reader, to
find that, since the books in the British Museum are catalogued
mainly according to their physical size, he had best work from the
catalogue. In the same way, one defensible arrangement of the
eighty-five MSS of the *Canterbury Tales* is according to the order of the
tales, a classification of major importance to the critic interested in
the unity of the tales, but only of peripheral importance to the
scholar interested solely in Chaucer's habits of composition or in his
language.

Before establishing a scheme of MSS, however, the editor must at
this stage view the available MSS in their textual relationship to each
other in order to establish the copy-text which will eventually
become the basic text of his edition. This process depends upon a
genealogical classification of the MSS involved, a task which in turn
demands that the editor first choose, by guess or God, a single MS as
a basis for the collation which will then serve as a basis for comparison and classification. This is the first of the apparently irreconcila-
ble "chicken or egg" problems the editor faces, and his first indica-
tion that no scientific method, no calculus, no battery of computers
can in the end take the place of what Housman meant by "art" and

45

what Donaldson calls the editor's "preconceptions—his learning, his taste, his experience, his judgment, his wisdom." [1]

I. COLLATION

This paradox of method, though logically insoluble, can be reduced with care and intelligence to a matter of expedient procedure. In general the literary student will seldom be faced with a group of absolutely virginal MSS; more than likely he will be re-editing rather than editing and can thus use as a basis for collation an already printed text. And lest he think such a procedure somehow "impure" or "unscholarly," let him consider that Manly and Rickert, who collated the 85 MSS of the *Canterbury Tales* in order to produce the "Chicago" edition, used Skeat's "Students' Edition" of the Oxford Chaucer, itself an eclectic rather than a critical text, as a basis for collation. The editor should also remember that in using a printed text he will probably be saved from the possibility of error in transcribing a working text at this point, though caution is always necessary.

Let us insert at this point a general caveat, perhaps obvious, but nevertheless vital. The editor cannot afford to become himself a scribe if he can avoid it. He should therefore not ever allow anyone, not even the most generous of assistants or the nicest of secretaries, to retype his text. He may white-out his errors, erase them, even cut them out of the paper with scissors if he must, but he must not ever retype a single line, much less a whole page, in order to correct an error.

Should there be no printed text readily available as a basis for collation, the editor had best *not* attempt to select on any qualitative basis the best MS to use. Appearances, particularly physical appearances, are deceiving, and the liquor-stained, poorly-written, late MS may in time offer the best text. It is a natural assumption that the most obviously expensive and carefully produced MS, say the Ellesmere *Canterbury Tales*, is the finest literary production, just as it is a natural assumption that the work for which the most MSS have survived was the most popular work of its time. Neither assumption, in spite of its superficial logic, is necessarily a true one. Better at this point for the editor to take the longest and most inclusive of the

MSS as a basis for collation and to reserve qualitative judgment until the collation itself affords a basis for choice.

If, and only if, the editor must make a transcription of a MS, should he now do so;[2] if he does not, he should proceed to the collation, realizing as he does so that, while it is a mechanical task, it is nevertheless worthy of his most careful attention. To rephrase Dr. Manly, let him not confuse minutiae with trifles.[3] There are a number of tested methods of collation ranging from columns on 14-inch legal pads to third generation computers.[4] Legal pads are notoriously cumbersome, however, and no matter how tempting and exotic the use of a computer may sound, the fledgling editor had best stick to a hand-done, mechanical system of collation, the simpler the better. In tasks like these, computers are nothing more than outrageously expensive automatic typewriters. They will not edit the text; they will only lay side by side the lines for comparison, a task which the editor himself can accomplish with a little drudgery, a great deal of care, and a decent-sized working surface. And as with any copying procedure, the use of a computer magnifies infinitely the possibility of error, especially when the operation is done by a bored and usually rushed programmer with no knowledge of or interest in the vagaries of Middle English spelling. The editor then will be faced with the problem of correcting his programmer's errors before setting out to make his own.

By far the easiest, fastest, most flexible, and most fool-proof system of collating multiple texts is that devised by Manly and Rickert.[5] Basically, though the editor will have to make his own adaptations, each line or appropriate lemma[6] of the text is copied at the top of a properly headed filing card. The $4'' \times 6''$ size, ruled, is recommended, since these cards are readily available, are small enough to be easily handled and filed in shoe boxes, and are wide enough to allow the editor to paste on each a facsimile of the line cut from a photographed copy of the printed text, thus avoiding the possibility of error in copying.

The MS designations, or sigla, are then listed down the side of the card, one line per MS, and any other cross-referring devices (tabs for grouping cards in various ways in the trays) are added. The editor can then begin to collate by listing under the appropriate word or

lemma and alongside the proper sigla the various MS forms or by striking out or circling the sigla of those MSS where no variant occurs. The editor is thus at a glance able to compare variants and to reconstruct the complete lemma from any given text. As Manly and Rickert point out, the editor may have to revise his lemmata occasionally in order to accommodate inversions or variant groupings, but generally once a card is established it becomes the single permanent, working record of variants. A sample card might thus look like this:[7]

```
line 1                                      The Corbin
lemma 1

          Once upon a midnight dreary,          Va1

            vp-on  midnyght                      Va2

                   dark nyght                    SLM

                        stormy,                  Ole MS

                   derk nyght                     AA

           Onc't   dark nyght                     UDC

                        dreary                    EAP
```

II. RECENSION

Collation completed, the editor must now choose the copy-text for the work, basing his decision on the type of edition he wishes to prepare. Once made, this decision is well-nigh irreversible. In general three broadly defined alternatives are open to the editor, although the possibilities of overlapping are almost infinite.

There is first of all the "diplomatic" edition, the faithfully transcribed reproduction as in a facsimile[8] of a single MS including every spelling variant, every mark of punctuation, every scribal error, no matter how obvious. In a diplomatic text, "the 'editing' is shown [only] in the annotations, the *suggested* emendations [in the notes], and the appending of the noteworthy divergent readings of other MSS." [9] Whatever the limitations of the diplomatic text, it at least involves a choice of copy-text based on some criterion of choosing a "best text."

The second text type, the "eclectic," does not demand the choice of a single copy-text, except perhaps for the singling out of that text

in which the editor will have to make the fewest number of changes. For in an extreme form the eclectic text is a composite work, a personal creation of the editor, a line from this text, a line from that, a word here, a word there. "The resultant text is, of course, smooth and musical, for artificial selection has been exercised with that end in view; but every student should understand that it is obtained by an intrusion of the editor's personal judgment between us and the author."[10] If one is a Tyrwhitt or a Skeat, the "resultant text" will bear witness to the judgment and knowledge and taste of a lifetime of scholarly activity; if one is a beginner, he had best refrain from eclecticism, lest, as Housman remarked in a different context, he "make a scarecrow of the author and a byword of himself." [11]

The last and generally preferable of the three is the "critical" edition, which is substantially an "edited" version of a "best" text. (The words in quotation are begged terms, and we know of no definition of either which would satisfy any two modern textual critics. But since this volume is a working manual rather than a philosophical treatise, rough definitions should be close enough, as we used to say, "for government work.") The modern critical edition began with the mid-nineteenth-century German scholar Karl Lachmann who, dissatisfied with the traditional eclecticism of editing classical texts, hit upon the "genealogical" method as a means of establishing the relationship between MSS, a process usually referred to as recension (*recensio*). The purpose of this complex process is to identify, if possible through comparison and elimination, the "archetype" (sometimes called the "original"),[12] the most primitive and therefore hopefully the most accurate extant text, the text from which all surviving MSS presumably derive.[13]

A basic authority here is a slim volume by Paul Maas called *Textual Criticism*.[14] Maas states early in his examination of the principles of recension that: "In what follows it is assumed (1) that the copies made since the primary split in the tradition each reproduce one exemplar only, i.e. that no scribe has combined several exemplars (*contaminatio*), (2) that each scribe consciously or unconsciously deviates from his exemplar, i.e. makes *'peculiar* errors.'"[15] But how often does either of these conditions of perfection exist in fact? As Talbot Donaldson has stated, a conscientious scribe might

well correct a reading in his exemplar "by glancing at a MS of a different family, or by searching his memory, or by simply using his intelligence" [16] thus contaminating by conflation the MS to a degree that, as Maas states, "the process of *eliminatio*[17] within the area of these 'contaminations' is greatly hindered, *if not made impossible*." [18] To consider the second of Maas's assumptions of regularity, in spite of Miss Hammond's statement that "no two scribes will show identical errors if working independently," [19] no scribe, conscientious or careless, can be counted on to make only errors peculiar to himself and never to duplicate errors of his counterpart in another monastery or scriptorium. For this "condition," as for his first, Maas has no remedy: "if a scribe does *not* deviate from his exemplar, *it is often impossible* to establish the relation of the witness [the MS in hand] to its exemplar and the other descendants of the exemplar." [20]

These objections to the genealogical method have been brought forward, not for the purpose of discrediting *a priori* the basis of what is surely the most widely accepted school of textual criticism, but in order that the editor may keep in mind as he reads how delicate an instrument is here described. For what passes in recension as science is in fact art and as such depends for its success upon the artistry of the editor rather than upon the accuracy of the method.

The purpose of recension is to establish a family tree, a stemma, of manuscripts by a comparison of their likenesses and differences on the basis of a collation already prepared. Let us take as an example the collation previously illustrated:[21]

line 1 lemma 1					The Corbin
	Once upon a midnight dreary,				Va^1
	$\check{v}$p-on	midnyght			Va^2
		dark nyght			SLM
			stormy,		Ole MS
		derk nyght			AA
	Onc't	dark nyght			UDC
			dreary		EAP

Proceeding on the basis of Maas's assumptions, a cursory comparison of the collation of this lemma reveals that viewed "horizontally" (and there is as yet no evidence for "vertical" conclusions) on the basis of substantive[22] and indicative variants, there are essentially three "family" groups—Va^1–Va^2–EAP (*midnight*), SLM–AA–UDC (*dark nyght*) and Ole MS (*stormy*). Before reaching any additional conclusions, however, the collation must be further examined:

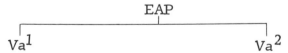

line 3 lemma 1		The Corbin
While I nodded, nearly napping	*plodded, nearly napping*	Va^1
When	no ddd nerely nap ping	Va^2
	nodded napping berely	SLM
	nodded barely napping	Ole MS
	nodded barely	AA
Then	nodded berely napping	UDC
While	nodded nearly napping	EAP

This lemma, first of all, corroborates the first horizontal grouping; on the basis of shared substantive variants, the families Va^1–Va^2—EAP (*nerely*), SLM–AA–UDC (*barely*) and Ole MS (*rarely*) remain constant. But Va^1 and Va^2, while sharing readings with EAP and containing no separative readings from the other two families, do contain unique readings (*plodded* in Va^1, *when* in Va^2) which set them apart from EAP, though not from the family. The editor is thus justified in assuming that Va^1 and Va^2 are derived from EAP and is ready for his first branching:

$$\text{EAP}$$
$$\overline{\quad\text{Va}^1 \qquad\qquad\qquad\qquad \text{Va}^2\quad}$$

Moreover, something of the same situation is developing in the other families. Ole MS remains unique with *rarely*, but SLM and UDC, like Va^1 and Va^2, while retaining their family characteristics do contain unique readings within the family (*then* in UDC, the inversion in SLM). Thus:

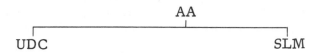

A later line introduces a further complication:

The editor is here faced for the first time with a crossing of family lines: Va^2 and UDC share the distinctive reading *black*. The assumption here is that one of the two scribes, let us say Va^2, consulted not only his exemplar EAP, but also UDC. This is an example, then, of conflation or contamination. Thus:

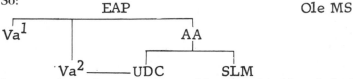

In the course of examining even these few cards the editor has perhaps made one further observation—not as yet demonstrable as fact, but definite enough to become a working hypothesis—that is, since EAP itself exhibits no unique substantive readings, it may well be the archetype of two of the three families, AA and the Va group, though (since Ole MS remains distinctive) not the author's original. So:

Let us end our demonstration at this point, for although further examination of the collation will result in further refinements of the

stemma, the principles of recension involved should at this point be clear.

It should be noted also that the editor has as a result of this recension established a new copy-text. EAP has replaced Va[1], and all other MSS, with the exception of the unique Ole MS, now exist simply in relation to it. If the editor does not keep his head at this point, what had appeared before to him to be simply variants may suddenly seem to be errors; indeed most of the genealogical critics (Maas for example[23]) had from the first so designated them. Here is another fallacy in the process of recension, though one which we have tried to avoid in our admittedly over-simplified example largely by using as indicative errors variants so distinctive as to obviate judgment. For, as Talbot Donaldson notes:

> It is always carefully pointed out that MSS may be grouped together only on the basis of shared error, but it is seldom pointed out that if an editor has to be able to distinguish right readings from wrong in order to evolve a stemma which will in turn distinguish right readings from wrong *for* him, then he might as well go on using this God-given power to distinguish right from wrong throughout the whole editorial process, and eliminate the stemma. The only reason for not doing so is to eliminate the appearance—not the fact—of subjectivity: the fact remains that the whole classification depends on purely subjective choices made before the work of editing begins.[24]

It should be noted that by arriving (through art, please note, not science) at a tentative identification of the archetype, though by no stretch of the imagination of the original, we have also arrived at the starting position of what James Thorpe[25] calls the "statistical" method, which was "invented" by Dom Henri Quentin, was refined by W. W. Greg, and is presently practiced by Vinton Dearing. Having attempted unsuccessfully to classify the various editions of the Vulgate by recension, Dom Quentin objected that the editor could not arrive at a "better" text simply by labelling variants as errors made by copyists from a lost original. Instead, by regarding variants simply as "formes diverses du textes," Dom Quentin thought he could "par une methode qui s'appuie sur des statisques rigoureuses" [26] determine the archetype.

Let us assume for the moment, therefore, that the previous collation had led only to the identification of the three family archetypes—EAP, AA, and Ole MS. In such a situation, the editor may actually edit statistically on the basis of his recension, the principle being that, where the MSS disagree, the majority rules and two against one (Dom Quentin's "iron rule") is decisive, even though such an assumption has a base neither in logic nor in fact and the two "sometimes agreed in nonsense while the one was making sense." [27]

Should his collation result in two, rather than three, family branches, the editor is thrown back again upon his own judgment as to the more authoritative of the branches, and it is precisely the frequency of this division of MSS into two families that led Professor Bedier to doubt the efficacy of editing by recension.[28] In 110 instances of recension examined by Bedier, 105 resulted in a division into two families—surely an alarming proportion, especially since the editor "discovers in the course of this work, and only then, as disclosures of the last moment, reasons to . . . simplify the tree." [29] (The fault, of course, lies not so much with the method, but with the editor's overreliance on it.) Bedier thus abandoned the whole genealogical method in favor of determining by other, more subjective tests—palaeographical, linguistic, literary—a "best" text, whether it proved to be the archetype or not.

At any rate, with EAP safely in hand, the process of editing becomes vastly simplified since, to quote Bowers, when the archetype "is preserved no other known manuscript can contain a reading that possesses any authority, although some may have readings that are more correct." [30] The editor is thus not excused from his editorial tasks—he must still search out errors—but he has at least a bench mark from which to start.

Since it is apparent that all three methods of determining a copy-text (genealogical, statistical, best-text) contain flaws both in theory and application, the editor is likely to throw up his hands in despair. Actually the situation is not that grave; all three methods have virtues as well as faults. By recension the editor can at least establish relationships; by statistics he can determine what may be correct readings; by the best-text method he can bring into play his own judgment and taste.

III. TRANSCRIPTION

Having selected a defensible copy-text, the editor is now faced with the problem of transcribing its manuscript. He would be well-advised to separate completely transcription from editing; unless a trustworthy diplomatic text exists, let him first transcribe and then edit, rather than edit as he goes along.

This does not mean, however, that the editor should not consider making certain minor changes in the text, dictated chiefly by typography, as he transcribes, providing that he decides on these changes *before* he begins transcribing in order to practice them consistently. Thus while he should not make any changes in the MS spelling, he might well transcribe þ and ð as *th* and ʒ as—well, who knows what.[31] He should also expand scribal abbreviations at this stage, carefully italicizing them, even though he may later wish to print them in Roman type. Many editors space and hyphenate words and supply punctuation at this stage, but these seem risky practices; since such matters may affect meaning, they are better left until the general editing.

IV. EMENDATION

A transcribed copy-text is thus not, save in a diplomatic edition, an edited text. Unless he chooses to retreat into sheer statistical analysis, the editor in emending the copy-text must constantly weigh rather than simply count the various MSS in the stemma, whatever their worth, in comparing them with his copy-text.[32] And even with the archetype in hand, decisions must be made; for no MS, whatever its authority, is faultless, nor can the MS itself be counted on to reveal its own errors: "To believe that wherever a best MS gives possible readings it gives true readings, and that only where it gives impossible readings does it give false readings, is to believe that an incompetent editor is the darling of Providence, which has given its angels charge over him." [33] In short, to quote James Willis:

> Here then is the final achievement demanded of the textual critic: that when he has established the reading best attested [presumably the copy-text] he must decide whether that reading is in fact what the author wrote; and if it is not, he must restore, if possible, what came from the author's pen. In deciding whether a reading is true or false, he balances probabili-

ties. . . . To assess these probabilities he must use, on the one side, his knowledge of the language, of the subject matter, and of the author's idiosyncrasies, and that sensitivity to language which detects the flat, the dull and the inartistic, not merely the ungrammatical, the unmetrical and the nonsensical; on the other side, his knowledge of scribes, their virtues and their vices, and all the causes, visual and psychological, of their wanderings from the truth.[34]

At this point, the editor should decide, even before reviewing the kinds of errors he is likely to encounter, upon some overall philosophy of emendation. There are two basically opposed approaches to the emending of literary manuscripts (between which there exist an infinite number of shadings)—that which aims at restoring the text to the state in which it was first delivered to the scribe, who is *ipso facto* an unreliable copyist, and that which refuses to allow personal judgments to override the editor's respect for the authority of the manuscript and of a scribe who, whatever his deficiencies, was closer to the event than even the most erudite modern scholar and who may have had before him an actual autograph. Both approaches have their advocates and their critics. The first can lead to excesses of personal taste, the second to the zenith, or depth, of editorial objectivity. James Willis presents the distinction sharply, along with its attendant dilemma:

The ultimate goal of conjectural criticism is to present what the author wrote, no matter how much the credit of the scribes may suffer; conservative criticism, in its extremest form, aims at proving that the manuscripts were always right. The successful defence of a manuscript reading pleases the conservative critic as a matter of principle; he must therefore, if he is to be consistent, welcome the successful defence of every suspected reading in a text. But if this goal is attained, and the attested readings are one and all accepted, what has the conservative critic in fact achieved? He has shown that the manuscript (either real or reconstructed) which conveyed the text of the work concerned contained no single error of any kind. Now it is almost certain that no such manuscript has ever existed. . . . What then of conjectural criticism? Has it not been guilty of crimes against grammar, metre, sense, and style as heinous as any that can be laid at the door of conservatism? It has indeed.[35]

In all probability, the best advice is to steer a middle course and, for the novice editor, perhaps the farther to starboard the better. Before making any change, the editor should (1) make every reasonable effort to justify the MS reading and (2) make no change without having a clear, articulate, and positive reason—linguistic, textual, palaeographical, whatever—for doing so.

What, then, are the types of scribal errors the editor can expect? The usual distinction is between "spontaneous" variation, i.e. "unconscious variation, perhaps a mere slip of the pen," and "determined" variation, "conscious, and hence usually an attempt at emendation (correct or not) of the copy being transcribed." [36] By far the greatest number of scribal errors fall into the first category; "mere slips of the pen" are so plentiful in fact that one distinguished modern editor, Eugene Vinaver, has discarded completely the genealogical method and has based an entire theory of classification and emendation on six types (of which five are clearly unconscious) of "emendable" errors made by scribes. [37] And while few critics might agree with Professor Vinaver's suggestions "as a substitute for more fundamental methods," [38] few would disagree with his assertion that a knowledge of the mechanics of scribal transcription may well provide a beginning means of separating scribal from authorial errors and hence a rational basis for some types of emendation. One must remember that the ability to check one document against another (which is what copying essentially is) as demonstrated by clerical aptitude tests is at least to some degree a natural talent and that the medieval scribe's working conditions and, in many cases, eyesight were far inferior to the modern editor's. Also, as H. J. Chaytor has shown, the scribe's habit of reading audibly caused him to make errors a visual reader would not make: "when the eye of a modern copyist leaves the manuscript before him in order to write, he carries in his mind a visual reminiscence of what he has seen. What the medieval scribe carried was an auditory memory, and probably in many cases, a memory of one word at a time." [39] The most common errors are thus:

I. Spontaneous errors:
    A. Simple confusion of letters or groups of letters, espe-

cially in those hands having similar letters (e.g. *c* and *e* in Carolingian minuscule and *c*, *t* and *u*, *v* in Gothic) and where the alteration of a single letter turns the MS word into an appropriate though incorrect substitute.

CT, B4045, *knew* for MS *krew*.
CT, D838, Koch (not quite a scribe!) reads *pace* for MSS *pees* or *pisse*.
CT, D1993, *ire* for MSS *hire*.
Pearl, 861, *lombe* for MS *lonbe*.
Pearl, 675, *face* for MS *fate*.

    B. Loss of letters or groups of letters:
        1. Haplography—the omission of a letter standing next to one similar.
CT, D210, *Love ye ther* for MSS *Love ther*, occasioned by resemblance of *y* and *þ*.
Pearl, 103, *feirer* for MS *feier*.

        2. Homoeoteleuton—literally "the same ending," the omission of a group of letters lying between similar groups, sometimes from one line to another.
CT, D313, *thogh that thow* for MSS *thogh thow*.
Pearl, 786, *forty fowre þowsande* for MS *forty þowsande*.

    C. Dittography—repetition of letters or groups of letters, sometimes from one line to another:
Pearl, 649, *out* for MS *out out*.
Pearl, 1063, *mynster* for MS *mynyster*.

    D. Transpositions of letters or groups of letters, most commonly in word order:
CT, A470, *Ne nevere yet no vileynye he sayde* for MS *He nevere yet no vileyne ne sayde*.
Pearl, 529, *þe date of day* for MS *þe day of date*.

    E. Incorrect division of letters or groups of letters, due largely to misunderstandings of abbreviations and punctuation:
Pearl, 154, *woþe þer* for MS *wo þer*.

    F. Errors in abbreviations:
CT, D193, *sire* for MSS *sires* where scribes mistook curl of *r* for *es* abbreviation.
Pearl, 436, *bygyner̄* for MS *bygyner*.
Purity, 692, *if* for MS *if̃*.

II. Determined Variations:

A. Attempts within a line to correct meter:
CT, D1584, *widwe* for MSS *wyf*

B. Attempts within a line to correct grammar:
CT, D852, *ben* for MSS *were*.

C. Attempts within a line to correct sense:
CT, D702, *faileth* for MSS *falleth* (an astrological term not understood by the scribes).

D. Interpolations—purposeful substitution, addition, or omission of whole passages for the sake of emending the sense or purpose of a passage:
CT, B3563–3652 in a number of MSS follow 3956.
CT, B1179, MSS read variously Somnour, Squyer, and Shipman.

One could go on, of course, to refine the list—for example, to distinguish between initial and final syllables omitted—but these errors are basically those which the editor can expect to find.[40] Having familiarized himself with the types of scribal errors he is likely to encounter, on what grounds then does the editor proceed to construct from his copy-text the critical text of his edition?

Continuing our hypothetical example, let us say that on the bases of collation and recension (1) the editor regards the original as lost, (2) he regards his copy-text (EAP) as the archetype of all except one MS, (3) he has other MSS (Ole MS, AA, Va¹, Va²) which, though derivative (except for Ole MS), may possibly provide useful readings, and (4) he has determined to steer a mid course between conservative and conjectural criticism, to respect the MS reading wherever he can justify it, but to change it where he feels that change does indeed restore these poems to their original forms. In short, he intends generally to pursue the aim of the textual critic as laid down by Fredson Bowers: "The aim of the textual critic, then, is: (1) the establishment of a text in its purest and most correct form, limited by the evidence of preserved documents; and (2) the application of techniques, including critical judgment, to clear a text of errors still present in the established, or documentary, form. The end of this second process is to approximate that correctness which would have appeared in an authorial fair copy of a text." [41]

It is perhaps time now for some exercises, which are in most cases

more demonstrations of the kinds of problems the editor can expect to find than "workable" exercises, though the student should at least try his hand at solutions (even though in many cases he will not have access to all the evidence, e.g., alternate MSS) before consulting the "answers," which are grouped at the end of the chapter. As noted earlier, generally accepted readings often have been deliberately altered or commonly rejected readings have been chosen in order to avoid the difficulties that would have resulted from selecting only editors' famous original emendations of cruces.

1.

Ryht so, ye ryche, yut rather ye sholde
Welcomen and worschipen and with youre good helpen
Godes munstrals and his mesagers and his mery bordiours,
The whiche arn lunatyk lordes and lepares aboute,
For under godes secret seal here synnes ben kevered.
  (*Piers Plowman*, C, X, 133–38)

2.

Thenne saw we a Samaritan, cam sittinge on a muyle,
Rydnge ful haply the right way we yeden,
Comynge fram a contreye that men callide Jerico,
To joust in Jerusalem he jaced awey ful faste.
  (*Piers Plowman*, C, XX, 47–50)

3.

For though myself be a ful vicious man,
A moral tale yet I yow telle kan,
Which Iames went to preche for to wynne.
Now hoold youre pees! my tale I wol bigynne.
  (*CT*, C459–62)

4.

(The Squire is describing Cambuskan's feast:)
Of which if I shal tellen al th'array,
Thanne wolde it occupie a someres day;

And eek it nedeth nat to devyse
At every cours the ordre of hire servyse.
   (*CT*, F63–66)

5.

(In commenting on Cambuskan's magic mirror, people:)
. . . speken of Alocen, and Vitulon,
And Aristotle, that writen in hir lyves
Of queynte mirours and of prospectives,
As knowen they that han hir bookes herd.
   (*CT*, F232–35)

6.

(A falcon is describing her false lover:)
   Right as a serpent hit hym under floures
Til he may seen his tyme for to byte,
Right so this god of love, ypocryte,
Dooth so his cerymonyes and obeisaunces,
And kepeth in semblaunt alle his observaunces
That sownen into gentillesse of love.
   (*CT*, F512–17)

7.

He lulleth hire, he kisseth hire ful ofte;
With thilke brustles of his berd unsofte,
Lyk to the skyn of houndfyssh, sharp as brere—
For he was shave al newe in his manere—
He rubbeth hire aboute hir tendre face . . . .
   (*CT*, E1823–27)

8.

Pluto . . .

. . .

Folwynge his wyf, the queene Proserpyna,
Which that he ravysheed out of Ethna
Whil that she gadered floures in the mede—

In Claudyan ye may the stories rede,
How in his grisely carte he hire sette—
This kyng of Fairye thanne adoun hym sette
Upon a bench of turves, fressh and grene,
And right anon thus seyde he to his queene . . . .
    (*CT*, E2227–36)

9.

(The death of Arcite:)
Out of the ground a fuyre infernal sterte,
From Pluto sent at requeste of Saturne,
For which his hors for fere gan to turne,
And leep aside, and foundred as he leep. . . .
    (*CT*, A2684–87)

10.

(The funeral of Arcite:)
The nobleste of the Grekes that ther were
Upon hir shuldres caryeden the beere,
With slakke paas, and eyen rede and wete,
Thurghout the citee by the maister strete,
That sprad was al with blak, and wonder hye
Right of the same is al the strete ywrye.
    (*CT*, A2899–904)

11.

Whanne þis werwolf was come to his wolnk denne,
  &hade brouȝt bilfoder for þe barnes mete,
Þat he hade wonne with wo wide wher a-boute,
Þan fond he nest & no neiȝ for nouȝt naȝ þer leued.
    whan þe best þe barn missed so balfully he ginneþ,
Þat alle men vpon molde no miȝt telle his sorwe. . . .
    (*William of Palerne*, 80–85)

12.

Whan melior þat meke mayde herd alisaundrines wordes,

&wiþ a sad sikyng seide to hire þanne
Sche was gretly gladed of hire gode bihest
A! curteyse cosyne crist mot þe it zelde
Of þi kynde cumfort þat þow me kuþest nowþe,
Þow hast warsched me wel wiþ þi mede wordes.
(*William of Palerne*, 599–605)

13.

Thenne watʒ hit lif vpon list to lyþen þe houndeʒ,
When alle þe mute hade hym met, menged togeder.
Suche a sorʒe at þat syʒt þay sette on his hede
As alle þe clamberande clyffes hade clatered on hepes. . . .
(*Sir Gawain and the Green Knight*, 1719–22)

14.

(Charlemagne approaches Narbonne:)
And þat cite he asseggede appone scre halfues,
While hym the ʒates were ʒette and ʒolden the keyes,
And Emorye made Emperour, even at that tyme,
To kepe it and to holde it to hym and to his ayres.
(*Parlement of the Three Ages*, 574–77)

15.

He lepeþ vp myd ydone
On a stede of faire bon.
He dassheþ forþ vpon þe londe,
Þe riche coroune on his honde
Of Nicholas þat he wan.
(*Kyng Alisaunder*, 1073–77)

16.

Mars was swiþe reed ferelyche;
Venus was þe saphire ylyche.
Mercurye he made gres-grene,
And Uouyne so metal shene.
(*Kyng Alisaunder*, 297–300)

17.

Þenne he swepe to þe sonde in sluchched cloþes—
Hit may wel be þat mester were his mantyle to wasche;
Þe bonk þat he blosched to, & bode hym bisyde,
Wern of regiounes ryȝt þat he renayed hade.
    (*Patience*, 341–44)

18.

Sir Kayous, sir Clegis with clene men of armes
Enconters them at the clyffe with clene men of armes,
Fyghttes faste in the fyrth, frythes no wapen,
Felled at the first come fyfe hundrethe at ones.
    (*Morte Arthure*, 2156–60)

19.

Mone makeles of mighte,
Þis is a nayre and a knyȝt,
Do him resone and riȝte,
For þi manhede.
    (*The Awntyrs off Arthure*, 348–51)

20.

Hit ȝaules, hit ȝameres, with wlonkes ful wete,
And seid withe siking sare:
"I bane þe body me bare;
Alas! now kindeles my care,
I gloppen and I grete."
    (*The Awntyrs off Arthure*, 87–91)

21.

Tweie gegges þe coupe bere;
So heui charged þat wroþ þai were.
Þai bad God ȝif him euel fin
Þat so mani floures dede þerin.
    (*Floris and Blauncheflor*, 178–80)

22.

And somme chosen to chaffare, þei chevide þe betere
As it semiþ to oure siȝt þat suche men þriven.
  (*Piers Plowman*, A, 31–32)

23.

And in the swete seson that swete is,
With a thred bastyng my slevis,
Alone I wente in my plaiyng,
The smale foules song harknyng. . . .
  (*The Romaunt of the Rose*, 103–106)

24.

As wisly as I sey the north-nor-west,
Whan I began my sweven for to write,
So yif me myght to ryme and ek t'endyte!
  (*The Parliament of Fowls*, 117–19)

And finally a whole poem from which to prepare a text, Chaucer's
Envoy to Scogan. First of all, here are Furnivall's transcriptions of the
three manuscript copies:

XIV. ENVOY TO SCOGAN.

THREE TEXTS, FROM

MS. Gg. 4. 27, in the University Library, Cambridge (*vellum*); FAIRFAX MS. 16, in the Bodleian Library, Oxford (*vellum*);

PEPYS 2006, in the Pepysian Library, Magdalene College, Cambridge (*paper*).

IN this late Poem, composd of two Terns and an Envoy, Chaucer,—hoar and round of shape (l. 31), 'Old Grizzle' as he calls himself (l. 35)—has shirkt the 'penance' of the Balade form, and not bothered himself with its same-rymes and refrain. The ruins alluded to in lines 11-14 were probably those of October 1393, as Mr Bradshaw and Prof. ten Brink both independently suggested.

The side-notes to l. 43-6—no doubt, Chaucer's own—are interesting as again bringing up Chaucer's connection with Kent, and with Greenwich, tho there he was then 'dull as death,' l. 45. (He was appointed on March 13, 1390, on a Commission with Sir Richard Stury[2], John Wadham, William Skrene, Henry Vanner, and John Culpepper, to repair the causeys, trenches, &c., on the banks of the Thames between the towns of Woolwich and Greenwich. Orig. 13 Rich. II, Roll xxx.)

The only 3 MS. copies of the poem that we have, seem to be all from one original, which Gg. 4. 27 most nearly represents. The two later MSS' change of *wellis* (fountains) to *stevene* in l. 43 must have been due to their scribes' desire of uniformity—that critic curse of varying Nature—with the *stevene* of l. 45; the transposition in l. 25 to whim, and mistake, like the Fairfax *thy* and *youre* of l. 25, 27.

Great thundering and lightning	[1] From Stowe's *Annales*, ed. 1605, p. 495:—
	"In September, lightnings and thunders, in many places of England did much hurt, but esp[e]cially in Cambridge-shire the same brent houses and corne neere to Tolleworke, and in the towne it brent terribly.
Grent water floods 1393	"Such aboundance of water fell in October, that at Bury in Suffolke, the Church was full of water, and at Newmarket it bare downe walles of houses, so that men and women hardly escaped drowning. The same yeere Lord Tho. de Ros, as he returned forth of the Holy land, in the city of Paphos, in the Ile of Cyprus, through intemperancy of the aire departed this life there § ". . .
	[2] One of the backers of the Wicliffites in 1395: see Stowe's *Annales* (1605), p. 499.

§ In 1394, according to Walsingham, died Isabel—Duchess of York, the wanton heroine of Chaucer's *Mars*—and her sister Constance, the second wife of John of Gaunt. On June 7, 1395, died Richard II's Queen, Anne of Bohemia, to whom Chaucer wanted

the second cast of his Prologue to the *Legende of Good Women* shown at Sheen. Stowe says, *Annales* (1605), p. 496:—

"The 'seventh of Iune, Queene Anne died at Shine in Southery [Surrey]. and was buried at Westminster. The King tooke her death so heauily, that, besides cursing-the place where she died, he did also for anger throwe downe the buildings vnto the which the former Kings, being wearied of the Citie, were wont for pleasure to resort.

"Thus the King, the Duke of Lancaster, and his sonne the Earle of Darbie, were widowers all at one time : for the Lady *Constance*, Dutchesse of Lancaster, daughter to Peter King of Spaine [see 'Chaucer's *Monk's Tale*'], was last lately deceased, whilest the Duke her husband was in France. And the same time also deceased the Countesse of Darby, wife to Henry, Earle of Darby. Moreouer, this yeere deceased *Isabel*, Dutches of Yorke, that was halfe sister to the Dutchess of Lancaster, being borne of one mother, and she was buried at Langley in the Frier Church there by the Kings commandment.

"Also this yeere [March 6, 1393] deceased that famous Knight known to the world, Sir *John Hawkwood*, whose deedes (saith Thomas Walsingham) require a speciall treatise [which Stowe gives]."

Queene Anne deceased *An. reg.* 18.	
[22 June 1394, to 21 June 1395] Constance Dutchesse of Lancaster deceased	
Sir John Hawkwood ; his acts. life anl death.	

Litera directa de Scogon per .G. C.

(1) *(Tern. I. 1)*   [¹ the in corrector's hand]

TO-brokene ben þe¹ statutis in heuene
þat creat were eternally to dure
Syn þat I se þe bryȝte goddis seuene
Mow wepe & wayle and passioun endure — 4
As may in erþe a mortal creature
Allas from whenns may þis þyng procede
Of whiche errour I deye almost for drede — 7

(2) *(I. 2)*   [² schape in corrector's hand]   [leaf 8]

Be word eterne whilhom was it schape²
þat from þe fifte serkele in no manere
Ne myȝte a drope of teeris doun escape
But now so wepyth venus in his spere — 11
þat wiþ hire teris sche wole drenche vs here
Allas skogon þis is for þyn offence
þu causist þis deluuye² of pestelence   [³ uye corrected] — 14

(3) *(L. 3)*

¶ Hast þu not seyd in blaspheme of þe godlis
þour pride or þour þyn grete recheles-nesse
Swich þyng as in þe lawe of loue forbodyn is
þat for þyn ladi saw not þyn distresse — 18
þerefore þou ȝeue hire vp at mychelmesse
Allas sogon of olde folke no þong
Was neuere erst Scogon blamyd for his tong — 21

¶ Lenvoy de Chauer A Scogan./

(1) *(Tern. I. 1)*

To-broken been the statutez / lye in Hevene
That creat weren / eternally to dure
Syth that I see / the bryght goddis seuene   [.i. vii. planete ./]
Mowe wepe and wayle / and passioun endure — 4
As may in erthe / a mortale creature
Allas fro whennes / may thys thinge procede
Of whiche errour / I deye almost for drede — 7

(2) *(I. 2)*

By worde eterne / whilcme was yshape — 8
That fro the fyfte sercle / in no maner
Ne myght a drope of teeres / doun eschape
But now so wepith venus / in hir spere — 11
That with hir teeres / she wol drenche vs here
Allas Scogan / this is for thyn offence
Thow cawsest this diluge / of pestilence — 14

(3) *(L. 3)*

Hauesthow not seyd / in blasphem of this godlis — 15
Thurgh pride / or thrugh they grete rekelnesse
Swich thing as in the lawe of love / forbede is
That for thi lady / sawgh nat thi distresse — 18
Therfore thow yave hire vp / at Mighelnesse
Allas Scogan / of olde folke ne yonge
Was neuer erst Scogan / blamed for his tonge — 21

¶ Lenuoie de Chaucer' A Scogan.

(1) *(Tern. I. 1)*

TO Broken ben the Statutȝ lye in heuen — 1
That creat were eternally to dure
Syn þat I se the bryght goldes seuene
Mow wepe and waile and passioñ endure — 4
As may in ȝerthe a mortaH creature
Alas fro hens may this thinge procede
Of which erroure I lye almoste for drede — 7

(2) *(L. 2)*

By worð eternð whilom was it shape — 8
That fro the fyfthe Cercle in no manere
Ne myght of terys douñ escape
But now so wepeth venus in here spere — 11
That wyth her' terys she woH drench vs here
Allas Scogañ this is for thirð offence
Thow causeste this diluge of pestilence — 14

(3) *(L. 3)*

Hastow not seið in blaspheme of the goddes — 15
Thourgh pride or þorow thi gret reklesnesse
Swich thinge as in þ˜ law of loue for-bede is
That for thi lady saugH nat thi distresse — 18
Therfore þou ȝafe here vp at Mighelnesse
Alas Scog˜ ñ of olð folk ne ȝonge
Was neuer er.t Scogañ blamed for his tonge — 21

(4) (*Tern* II. 1)

¶ þow drow in scorn cupid ek to record
Of þe ilke rebel word þat þou hast spoken
For whiche he wele no lengere be þyn lord
And þow his bowe Scogon benot broken
He wil not with his arwis ben I-wroken
On þe ne me ne none of oure figure
We schal of him haue neyþer hurt ne cure

(5) (II. 2)

¶ Now sertys frend I drede of thyn onhap
Lest for þyn gilt þe wreche of loue procede
On alle hem þat ben hore & round of schap
þat ben so likly folk in loue to spede
þanne schal we for oure labour han no mede
But wel I wit þou wilt answere & seye
Lo olde grisil leste to ryme & pleye

(6) (II. 3)

¶ Nay Scogon sey not so for I me excuse
God helpe me so in no rym douteles
Ne þynke I neuere of slep to wake myn muse
þat rustyþ in myn schede stylle in pes
Whil I was ȝong I putte it forþ in pres
But al schal passyn þat men prose or ryme
Tak euery man his torn as for his tyme

(7) (*Lenvoy*)

Scogan þat knelist at þe wellis hed [leaf 8, back]
Of grace of alle honour and worþynesse .i. Wyndisore
In þe ende of wich strem I am dul as ded [s. *corr.*]
Forgete in solitarie wildirnes .i. a Grenewych
ȝit Scogan þyng on tullius kyndenes
Mynewe þyn frend þere it may fructifie
Farewel & loke þou neuere eft loue defye

(4) (*Tern* II. 1)

Thow drowe in skorne / Cupide eke to recorde
Of thilke rebel worde / that thow hast spoken
For which he wol no lenger / be thy lorde
And Scogan thow thy bowe / be nat broken
He wol nat with his Arwes / been y-wroken [leaf 193]
On the ne me / ne noon of youre Figure
We shul of him haue / neyther hurte nor cure

(5) (II. 2)

Now certes frend / I dreed of thyn vnhappe
Leste for thy gilte / the wreche of love procede
On alle hem that ben hoor / and rounde of shappe
That ben so lykly folke / in loue to spede
Than shal we for oure laboure / haue noo mede
But wel I wot / thow wolt answere and saye
Loo tholde grisel lyste / to Ryme and playe

(6) (II. 3)

Nay Scogan say not soo / for I mexcuse
God helpe me soo / in no Ryme dowteles
Ne thynke I neuer of slepe / to wake my muse
That rusteth in my shethe / stille in pees
While I was yonge / I put hyt forth in prees
But alle shal passe / that men prose or ryme
Take euery man hys turne / as for his tyme

(7) (*Envoy*)

Scogan that knelest / at the stremes hede .i. a Wyndesor
Of grace / of alle honour and worthynesse
In thende of which streme / I am dul . as dede
Forgete / in solytarie wildernesse .i. a Grenewich
Yet Scogan / thenke on Tullius kyndenesse
Mynne thy frend / there it may fructyfye
Fare wel / and loke thow neuer eft / loue dyffye

(4) (*Tern* II. 1)

Thow drow in scorn Cupide ek to record
Of thilk rebell word þat thow haste spoken
For which he will no lenger be thi lord
And Scogan þough his bowe be not broken
He will not wyth his arowes ben ywroken
On þe / ne me / no non of owre figure
We shull of hem han neþer hurt ne cure.

(5) (II. 2)

Now certes frend I drede of thin vnhape [page 386]
Lest for thi gilte þe wreche of loue procede
On all hem þat ben hore and round of shape
That ben so likly folk to spede
Than we shull for our labour han no mede
But well I wot thow wyll answere and seye
Lo olde grysell liste to ryme and play

(6) (II. 3)

Nay Scogan sey not so for I mexcuse
God help me so in no ryme doutheles
Ne thinke I neuer of slepe wake my Muse
That rusteth in my shethe still in pes
While I was yonge I put her forth in pres
But all shall passe that men prose or ryme
Take euery man his turn as for his tymee

(7) (*Envoy*)

Scogan that kneliste at the stremes hede **A Windesore**
Of grace of all honour and worthinesse
In the Ende of wych streme I am dull as ded **A Grenwich**
Forgete in solitarye wyldernesse
Yet Scogan thenk on Tullius kindnesse
Mynne thi frend þer it may fructifye
Fare well and loke þou neuer eft loue defye.

Next, in black letter, a reproduction of Thynne's text of 1532:

Balades.   **fo. CCC. lxxxii.**

TO broken ben the statutes hye i heuen
That create were eternally tendure
Sithe that I se the bright goddes seuen
Mowe wepe and wayle / and passyon endure
As may in erthe a mortal creature
Alas / fro whense may this thyng procede
Of whiche errour I dye almost for drede

By worde eterne whilom was it shape
That fro the fyfth cercle in no manere
Ne myght of teares downe escape
But nowe so wepeth Venus in her sphere
That with her teares she wol drench vs here
Alas Scogan this is for thyne offence
Thou causest this deluge of pestylence

Hast thou nat sayd in blaspheme of y goddis
Through pryde / or through thy gret rekelnesse
Such thyngs as in the lawe of loue forbode is
That for thy lady sawe nat thy distresse
Therfore thou yaue her vp at Myghelmesse
Alas Scogan of olde folke ne yonge
Was neuer erst Scogan blamed for his tong

Thou drewe in scorne Cuppde eke to recorde
Of thilke rebel worde y thou haste spoken
For whiche he wol no lenger be thy lorde
And Scogan / though his bowe be nat broken
He wol nat with his arowes ben ywroken
On the ne me / ne none of our fygure
We shal of him haue neither hurte ne cure

Nowe certes frende I drede of thyne vnhappe
Lest for thy gylte the wreche of loue procede
On al hem that ben hore & rounde of shappe
That ben so lykely folke to spede
Than we shal for our labour haue our mede
But wel I wotte thou wolt answere & say
Lo olde grysel lyste to renne and play

Nay Scogan say nat so / for I me excuse
God helpe me so / in no ryme douteles
Ne thynke I neuer of slepe wake my muse
That rusteth in my sheth styl in pees
While I was yonge I put her forth in prees
But al shal passe that men prose or ryme
Take euery man his tourne as for his tyme

Scogan thou knelest at the stremes heed
Of grace / of al honour / and of worthynesse
In thende of whiche I am dul as deed
Forgoten in solytary wyldernesse
Yet Scogan thynke on Tullius kyndnesse
Mynne thy frende there it may fructify
Farewel / and loke thou neuer efte loue defy
¶ Explicit.

OD forthe kyng / rule the by sapience
Bisshoppe be able to mynister doctrine
Lorde to trewe counsayle yeue audience
Womanhede to chastyte euer enclyne
Knyght lette thy dedes worship determyne
Be rightous iuge in sauyng thy name
Rich do almesse / lest thou lese blysse wt shame

People obey your kyng and the lawe
Age be thou ruled by good relygion
Trewe seruant be dredeful & kepe y vnder awe
And thou poore spye on presumption
Inobedience to youth is vtter distruction
Remembre you howe god hath set you so
And do your parte as ye be ordayned to.

¶ Chaucer vnto his empty purse.
To you my purse and to non other wight
Complayne I / for ye be my lady dere
I am sorye nowe that ye be lyght
For certes ye nowe make me heuy chere
Me were as lefe be layde vpon a bere
For whiche vnto your mercy thus I crye
Be heuy agayne or els mote I dye

Nowe vouchsafe this day or it be nyght
That I of you the blyssful sowne may here
Or se your colour lyke the sonne bright
That of yelownesse had neuer pere
Ye be my lyfe / ye be my hertes stere
Quene of conforte and of good company
Be heuy agayne / or els mote I dye

Nowe purse that arte to me my lyues lyght
And sauyour / as downe in this worlde here
Out of this towne helpe me by your myght
Sithe that ye wol nat be my tresourere
For I am shaue as nyghe as any frere
But I pray vnto your curtesye
Be heuy agayne / or els mote I dye.
¶ Explicit.

Next, Skeat's text and notes (The Oxford Chaucer - 1899):

XVI. LENVOY DE CHAUCER A SCOGAN.

To-broken been the statuts hye in hevene
That creat were eternally to dure,
Sith that I see the brighte goddes sevene
Mow wepe and wayle, and passioun endure,
As may in erthe a mortal creature. 5
Allas, fro whennes may this thing procede?
Of whiche errour I deye almost for drede.

By worde eterne whylom was hit shape
That fro the fifte cercle, in no manere,
Ne mighte a drope of teres doun escape. 10
But now so wepeth Venus in hir spere,
That with hir teres she wol drenche us here.
Allas, Scogan! this is for thyn offence!
Thou causest this deluge of pestilence.

Hast thou not seyd, in blaspheme of this goddes, 15
Through pryde, or through thy grete rakelnesse,
Swich thing as in the lawe of love forbode is?
That, for thy lady saw nat thy distresse,
Therfor thou yave hir up at Michelmesse!
Allas, Scogan! of olde folk ne yonge 20
Was never erst Scogan blamed for his tonge!

TITLE : *so in* F. *and* P.; Gg. *has*—Litera directa de Scogon per G. C.
The MSS. *are*: Gg. (Camb. Univ. Library, Gg. 4. 27); F. (Fairfax 16); P.
(Pepys 2006). Th. = Thynne (1532). *I follow* F. *mainly.*
1. F. statutez. 2. F. weren eternaly. 3. F. bryght goddis. 4.
F. Mowe. 5. F. Mortale. 6. F. thys thinge. 8. F. whilome. F.
yshape; Gg. it schape; P. Th. it shape. 9. F. fyfte sercle; maner. 10. F.
myght; teeres; eschape. 11. F. wepith. 12. F. teeres. 14. F.
cawsest; diluge. 15. Gg. Hast þu; F. Hauesthow. F. this goddis; Gg. the
goddis; P. Th. the goddes. 16. F. Thurgh; thrugh. F. they (*wrongly*);
Gg. þyn; P. thi. F. rekelnesse; P. Th. reklesnesse ; Gg. rechelesnesse; *see* note.
17. F. P. forbede; Gg. forhodyn; Th. forbode. 18. Gg. saw; F. sawgh.
19. F. Therfore thow. Gg. Mychel-; F. Mighel-. 20. F. folke.

Thou drowe in scorn Cupyde eek to record
Of thilke rebel word that thou hast spoken,
For which he wol no lenger be thy lord.
And, Scogan, thogh his bowe be nat broken,   25
He wol nat with his arwes been y-wroken
On thee, ne me, ne noon of our figure ;
We shul of him have neyther hurt ne cure.

Now certes, frend, I drede of thyn unhappe,
Lest for thy gilt the wreche of Love procede   30
On alle hem that ben hore and rounde of shape,
That ben so lykly folk in love to spede.
Than shul we for our labour han no mede ;
But wel I wot, thou wilt answere and seye :
'Lo ! olde Grisel list to ryme and pleye !'   35

Nay, Scogan, sey not so, for I mexcuse,
God help me so ! in no rym, doutelees,
Ne thinke I never of slepe wak my muse,
That rusteth in my shethe stille in pees.
Whyl I was yong, I putte hir forth in prees,   40
But al shal passe that men prose or ryme ;
Take every man his turn, as for his tyme.

Envoy.

Scogan, that knelest at the stremes heed
Of grace, of alle honour and worthinesse.
In thende of which streme I am dul as deed,   45
Forgete in solitarie wildernesse ;
Yet, Scogan, thenke on Tullius kindenesse,
Minne thy frend, ther it may fructifye !
Far-wel, and lok thou never eft Love defye !   49

---

22. F. skorne; eke; recorde.   23. F. worde; thow.   24. F. lorde.
25. F. thow; P. Th. though.   F. thy (*for* his, *wrongly*); Gg. P. his.   27. F.
the. Th. our; Gg. oure; P. owre; F. youre.   28. F. hurte. Gg. P. Th. ne ;
F. nor.   29. F. dreed.   30. F. gilte.   31. Gg. P. hore; F. hoor. F. shappe ;
P. shape; Gg. schap.   32. F. folke.   33. P. shull; F. Gg. shal. Gg. P.
han; F. haue. F. noo.   34. F. thow. F. wolt; Gg. wilt.   35. Gg. P.
Lo olde; F. Loo tholde. F. lyste.   36. F. say; Gg. P. sey. F. soo.   37.
P. help; Gg. F. helpe. F. soo. F. ryme dowteles.   38. F. Gg. to wake; P.
Th. *om.* to.   40. F. While; yonge. Gg. putte; F. put. P. Th. her; F. hyt;
Gg. it.   41. F. alle.   42. F. hys turne.   43. F. hede; Gg. hed.   45. F.
dede; Gg. P. ded.   48. F. Mynne; there.   49. F. Fare; loke thow; dyffye.
N.B. *All have* —.i. a Windesore, *and* — .i. a Grenewich *opposite* ll. 43, 45.

XVI. Lenvoy a Scogan.

THERE are but three MSS., all much alike. As to Scogan, see the Introduction. MSS. F. and P. have the heading—'Lenvoy de Chaucer a Scogan'; Gg. has—'Litera directa de Scogon per G. C.'

1, 2. These two lines are quite Dantesque. Cf. Purg. i. 47, 76 ; Inf. iii. 8 :—'Son le leggi . . . cosi rotte'; 'gli editti eterni . . . guasti'; 'io eterno duro.'

3. The 'seven bright gods' are the seven planets. The allusion is to some great floods of rain that had fallen. Chaucer says it is because the heavenly influences are no longer controlled ; the seven planets are allowed to weep upon the earth. The year was probably 1393, with respect to which we find in Stowe's Annales, ed. 1605, p. 495 :— 'In September, lightnings and thunders, in many places of England did much hurt, but esp[e]cially in Cambridge-shire the same brent houses and corne near to Tolleworke, and in the Towne it brent terribly. Such abundance of water fell in October, that at Bury in Suffolke the church was full of water, and at Newmarket it bare downe walles of houses, so that men and women hardly escaped drowning.' Note the mention of Michaelmas in l. 19, shewing that the poem was written towards the close of the year.

7. *Errour*; among the senses given by Cotgrave for F. *erreur* we find ' ignorance, false opinion.' Owing to his ignorance, Chaucer is almost dead for fear ; i. e. he wants to know the reason for it all.

9. *Fifte cercle*, fifth circle or sphere of the planets, reckoning from without ; see note to Mars, l. 29. This fifth sphere is that of *Venus*.

14. *This deluge of pestilence*, this late pestilential flood. There were several great pestilences in the fourteenth century, notably in 1348-9, 1361-2, 1369, and 1375-6; cf. note to IV. 96. Chaucer seems to imply that the bad weather may cause another plague.

15. *Goddes*, goddess, Venus ; here spoken of as the goddess of *love*.

16. *Rakelnesse*, rashness. The MSS. have *rekelnesse, reklesnesse, rechelesnesse* ; the first is nearly right. *Rakelnesse* is Chaucer's word, Cant. Tales, 17232 (H 283) ; five lines above, Phœbus blames his *rakel hond*, because he had slain his wife.

17. *Forbode is* ; rather a forced rime to *goddes* ; see p. 488 (note).

21. *Erst*, before. I accept Chaucer's clear evidence that his friend Scogan (probably Henry Scogan) was not the same person as the John (or Thomas) Scogan to whom various silly jests were afterwards attributed.

22. *To record*, by way of witness. *Record*, as Koch remarks, is here a sb., riming with *lord* ; not the gerund *record-e*.

27. *Of our figure*, of our (portly) shape ; see l. 31.

28. *Him*, i. e. Cupid. The Pepys MS. has *hem*, them, i. e. the arrows. Koch reads *hem*, and remarks that it makes the best sense. But it comes to much the same thing. Cf. Parl. of Foules, 217, where some of Cupid's arrows are said to slay, and some to wound. It was the spear of Achilles that could both wound and cure ; see Squi. Tale,

F 240, and the note. Perhaps, in some cases, the arrow of Cupid may be supposed to cure likewise ; but it is simpler to ascribe the cure to Cupid himself. Observe the use of *he* in ll. 24 and 26, and of *his* in ll. 25 and 26. Thynne has *hym*.

29. *I drede of*, I fear for thy misfortune.

30. *Wreche*, vengeance; distinct from *wrecche*.

31. 'Gray-headed and round of shape'; i.e. like ourselves. Cf. what Chaucer says of his own shape ; C. T. Group B, 1890.

35. 'See, the old gray-haired man is pleased to rime and amuse himself.' For *ryme* (as in the three MSS.), the old editions have *renne*. This would mean, ' See, the old gray horse is pleased to run about and play.' And possibly this is right ; for the O. F. *grisel* properly means a gray horse, as shewn in Godefroy's O. F. Dict.

36. *Mexcuse*, for *me excuse*, excuse myself. Cf. *mawreke*, Compleint to Pite, 11.

43. For *stremes*, Gg. has *wellis*; but the whole expression *stremes heed* is equivalent to *well*, and we have *which streme* in l. 45 (Koch).

In the MSS., the words *stremes heed* are explained by *Windesore* (Windsor), and *ende of whiche streme* in l. 45 by *Grenewich* (Greenwich) ; explanations which are probably correct. Thus the *stream* is the Thames ; Chaucer was living, in a solitary way, at Greenwich, whilst Scogan was with the court at Windsor, much nearer to the source of favour.

47. *Tullius*. Perhaps, says Koch, there is an allusion to Cicero's Epist. vi. ad Cæcinam. For myself, I think he alludes to his De Amicitia ; see note to Rom. Rose, 5286.

The Globe text (1898) and notes:

LENVOY DE CHAUCER A SCOGAN

To-BROKEN been the statutes hye in hevene,
That crëat were eternally to dure,
Sith that I see the bryghtë goddés sevene
Mowe wepe and wayle, and passioun endure,
As may in erthe a mortale crëature.
Allas ! fro whennés may this thing pro-
cede ?
Of whiche errour I deye almost for drede.

By worde eterne whilom was it y-shape,
That fro the fiftë cercle, in no manére,
Ne myghte a drope of terés doun eschape.
But now so wepeth Venus in hir spere, 11
That with hir terés she wol drenche us here.
Allas, Scogan ! this is for thyn offence !
Thou causest this deluge of pestilence.

Hast thou not seyd in blaspheme of this goddés,
Through pride, or through thy gretë rekelnesse,
Swich thing as in the lawe of love forbode is ?
That, for thy lady saw nat thy distresse,
Therfor thou yave hir up at Michelmesse?
Allas, Scogan ! of oldé folk ne yonge, 20
Was never erst Scogan blaméd for his tonge.

4. *wepe and wayle*. Probably a reference to the heavy rains and floods of 1393.

5. Ct. F Harl. 7578 *Is no thing lyke;* Add. *Ar nothing like.*

10. Tr. Th. Ct. F Add. Harl. 7578 *For amonge us;* Bann. *Among us now.*

17. Harl. 7578 Ct. F *man* for *wyght.*

28. Harl. 7578 Ct. F Tr. Th. *And wed.*

Thou drowe in scorn Cupide eek to
recorde
Of thilké rebel word that thou hast spoken,
For which he wol no lenger be thy lord.
And, Scogan, thogh his bowé be nat
broken,
He wol nat with his arwés been y-wroken
On thee, ne me, ne noon of our figure ;
We shul of him have neyther hurte ne cure.

Now certés, frend, I drede of thyn
unhappe,
Leste for thy gilte the wreche of love
procede   3c
On alle hem that ben hore and rounde of
shape,
That ben so lykly folk in love to spede.
Than shul we for our labour han no mede ;
But wel I wot, thou wilt answere and seye,
' Loo, tholdé Grisel list to ryme and pleye!'

Nay, Scogan, say not so, for I mexcuse,
God helpe me so ! in no ryme doutélees,
Ne thynke I never of sleep to wake my
muse,   38
That rusteth in my shethé stille in pees ;
While I was yong I put hir forth in prees ;
But al shal passén that men prose or ryme,
Take every man his turne as for his tyme.

ENVOY

Scogan, that knelest at the stremés hede
Of grace, of alle honour, and worthy-
nesse !
In thende of which streme I am dul as
dede,
Forgete in solitarie wildernesse ;
Yet, Scogan, thenke on Tullius kyndé-
nesse ;
Mynné thy frend ther it may fructifye,
Far-wel, and lok thou never eft love defye.

And finally the text and notes of F. N. Robinson (1957):

Lenvoy de Chaucer a Scogan

Tobroken been the statutz hye in hevene
That creat were eternally to dure,
Syth that I see the bryghte goddis sevene
Mowe wepe and wayle, and passion endure,
As may in erthe a mortal creature.   5
Allas, fro whennes may thys thing procede,
Of which errour I deye almost for drede?

By word eterne whilom was yshape
That fro the fyfte sercle, in no manere,
Ne myghte a drope of teeres doun escape.   10
But now so wepith Venus in hir spere
That with hir teeres she wol drenche us here.
Allas! Scogan, this is for thyn offence;
Thow causest this diluge of pestilence.   14

Hastow not seyd, in blaspheme of the goddes,
Thurgh pride, or thrugh thy grete rekelnesse,
Swich thing as in the lawe of love forbode is,
That, for thy lady sawgh nat thy distresse,
Therfore thow yave hir up at Michelmesse?
Allas! Scogan, of olde folk ne yonge   20
Was never erst Scogan blamed for his tonge.

Thow drowe in skorn Cupide eke to record
Of thilke rebel word that thou hast spoken,
For which he wol no lenger be thy lord.
And, Scogan, though his bowe be nat broken,
He wol nat with his arwes been ywroken   26
On the, ne me, ne noon of oure figure;
We shul of him have neyther hurt ne cure.

Now certes, frend, I dreede of thyn unhap,   29
Lest for thy gilt the wreche of Love procede
On alle hem that ben hoor and rounde of shap,
That ben so lykly folk in love to spede.
Than shal we for oure labour han no mede;
But wel I wot, thow wolt answere and saye:
"Lo, olde Grisel lyst to ryme and playe!"   35

Nay, Scogan, say not so, for I m'excuse —
God helpe me so! — in no rym, dowteles,
Ne thynke I never of slep to wake my muse,
That rusteth in my shethe stille in pees.
While I was yong, I put hir forth in prees;   40
But al shal passe that men prose or ryme;
Take every man hys turn, as for his tyme.

Envoy

Scogan, that knelest at the stremes hed
Of grace, of alle honour and worthynesse,
In th'ende of which strem I am dul as ded,   45
Forgete in solytarie wildernesse, —
Yet, Scogan, thenke on Tullius kyndenesse;
Mynne thy frend, there it may fructyfye!
Far-wel, and loke thow never eft Love dyffye.

Lenvoy de Chaucer a Scogan

Authorities: three MSS.: Gg 4. 27 (Gg) of the
Cambridge University Library, Fairfax 16 (F) of the
Bodleian, and Pepys 2006 (P) of Magdalene College, Cambridge; and the editions of Caxton, 1477–
78 (Cx), first three stanzas only, and of Thynne,
1532 (Th). The first four copies have been printed
by the Chaucer Society; Th is available in Skeat's
facsimile edition. There is no clear evidence for a
classification of the MSS. Cx and Th correspond
most nearly to P. The three MSS. are of about equal
value; F is taken as the basis of the present text.

15 *the goddes*] *this goddis* F only.
16 *rekelnesse* F Th; *rek(e)lesnes(se)* Gg P Cx;
probably for *rakelnesse.*

28 *him* F Gg Th; *hem* P (possibly correctly, referring to the arrows).

L'envoy de Chaucer a Scogan

The *Envoy* is attributed to Chaucer in all three MSS., Gg. 4. 27, Fairfax 16, and Pepys 2006, and generally accepted as authentic.

Scogan is generally held to have been Henry Scogan (1361?–1407), lord of the manor of Haviles after the death of his brother, John Scogan, in 1391. He became tutor to the sons of Henry IV, and his only literary work is the "Moral Balade" addressed to them and written after the death of Chaucer. In that poem he quotes the entire text of *Gentilesse*, and refers to Chaucer several times as his "maistre."

Chaucer's *Envoy* is supposed to have been written in 1393, toward the end of the year (after Michaelmas, l. 19). The *diluge of pestilence* (l. 14) may well refer to the great floods of rain which fell in September and October. See Stowe's Annales, London, 1631, p. 308 (quoted in Skeat's notes), and Walsingham, Historia Anglicana, ed. Riley, London, 1863–64, II, 213. At that time Scogan was only thirty-two years of age, and Chaucer's association of him with those that are too old for love must not be taken very seriously. On this matter, and on the (erroneous) attribution of the Court of Love to Scogan, see Kittredge, [Harv.] Stud. and Notes, I, 109 ff.

Both the identity of Scogan and the date of the *Envoy*, it should be added, have been called in question by Professor Brusendorff (pp. 289 ff.). He proposed to explain the deluge as a reference to a prolonged period of dampness and pestilence recorded by Walsingham (II, 202 f.) for the summer of 1391. Scogan, he held, was not Henry but his elder brother John, who died in 1391, perhaps a victim of the pestilence. But there is no strong reason for applying the poem to the conditions of 1391 rather than 1393, and the argument that John Scogan's age fits the description (ll. 31–32) better than Henry's counts for little in view of the manifestly humorous tone of the passage. Moreover there is no such evidence of John Scogan's association with Chaucer as is furnished in Henry's case by his Moral Balade.

1–2 With these lines have been compared two passages.in Dante's Purgatorio (i, 46 and 76). But it may be questioned whether the broken statutes here were suggested by the "leggi rotte" of the pit.

3 *the bryghte goddis sevene,* the planets. On their relation to the floods see R. K. Root, PMLA, XXXIX, 59.

7 *errour,* probably the aberration or abnormality of the weather rather than the ignorance of the poet (as suggested by Skeat).

9 *the fyfte sercle*, the sphere of Venus.

14 *diluge of pestilence*, pestilential deluge. For the construction cf. *KnT*, I, 1912, n.

15 *the goddes*; Skeat reads *this goddes*, "this goddess," i.e., Venus. But the form *goddes* for *goddesse* in rime is hardly Chaucerian.

21 *erst*, before. For this idiomatic use of the superlative see *KnT*, I, 1566, n.

28 Cf. RR, 1876 ff.

35 *Grisel*, "the old gray-haired man"; or, if the reading *renne* be adopted for *ryme*, "the gray horse."

38–39 The figure is perhaps from the Anticlaudianus of Alanus de Insulis, close of the prose preface and l. 3 of the verse preface (Migne, Pat. Lat., CCX, 487–88). Alanus, Professor Kittredge has pointed out to the editor, may in turn have been echoing Ovid's Tristia, v, 12, 21 f.

43 *the stremes hed*, marked "Windesore" in the MSS. Similarly, l. 45 is written "Grenewich" (Chaucer's residence). But Professor Manly (New Light, pp. 40 f.) argues that Chaucer was probably living at North Petherton in 1393. The marginal reference to Windsor, he suggests, may date from the time of Henry VI, who spent much time there.

47 It is uncertain what is meant by what the editors have taken to be a reference to Cicero. They have referred to Epist. vi, ad Caecinam, and to the De Amicitia. But it is possible, as Professor R. C. Goffin has pointed out (MLR, XX, 318 ff.), that Chaucer was quoting "Tullius" at second hand and really had in mind the citations on "love of friendship" in RR, 4747 ff. (*Rom*, 5285 ff.). For the not improbable suggestion that Chaucer is referring to the generosity of Tullius Hostilius, see T. M. Phipps, MLN, LVIII, 108.

From this collection of sources, the editor should be able to prepare an edition—diplomatic, eclectic, or critical—of the *Lenvoy de Chaucer a Scogan* complete with apparatus and notes. For the glossary he will have to step outside of the present text.

But perhaps before he does so, he had best read a little farther.

SOLUTIONS TO PROBLEMS
ON PAGES 58 THROUGH 63

1

For *lordes* read either *loreles*, vagabonds, or possibly *lollares*, idlers (Skeat), but on no account *lordes* who are not minstrels or jesters.

2

Since the alliterative pattern in l. 2 is likely determined by *rydynge* and *right*, *haply* should certainly be *raply*, quickly.

3

Iames went, though appearing in thirteen MSS (all of a single group), is obviously incorrect. The better MSS read *I am wont*.

4

Line 3 is metrically deficient, and a number of MSS read *for to*, a grammatically interchangeable construction, in order to complete the line.

5

Prospectives, which makes little sense, could easily result from a misreading of the abbreviation for *perspectives* (ꝓ for ꝑ).

6

The falcon would hardly refer to her treacherous lover as a god of love. The best MSS read *this god of loves ypocrite*.

7

In spite of the fact that the more authoritative MSS (El and Hg, for example) read *thilke* (l. 2), the close resemblance between *lk* and *kk* permits *thikke*, surely a better reading.

8

F and *s* being almost indistinguishable coupled with the fact that Chaucer's "identical rhymes never admit of two words with exactly the same construction and meaning" makes *he hire fette* almost certainly the correct reading.

9

The MSS are divided between *fuyre* (l. 1) and *furye*. The source (*La Teseide*, IX, 4–7) makes it clear that Pluto sent a fury, not a fire.

10

In the last line, *al* is superfluous since the final *e* in *same*, preceding
as it does the caesura, was probably pronounced. *Al* could have been
picked up from the preceding line.

11

The MS reads *ginneþ*, but with no verb following. The editor must
supply a verb (e.g. *ginneþ greve*) or emend to *grinneþ*, as does Skeat.

12

The transposition of ll. 2 and 3 is obvious.

13

Lif vpon list makes no sense; the proper emendation of nearly all
editors is *list vpon lif*. The transposition was natural due to the
similarity of *s* and *f*.

14

A second MS demonstrates that *to have and to holde it* is the proper
reading of the last line. Even without such help, however, the
alliterative pattern and the frequency of "to have and to hold" in ME
verse would justify the emendation.

15

The French phrase *faire bon* makes little sense; an alternate MS
supplies *Nerebone*. Obviously the scribe made an auditory error,
typical, by the way, of the so-called Lincoln's Inn MS of this poem.

16

Since the poet is here making specific comparisons in terms of
graphic images, *reed fere lyche*, red like a fire, is surely a better reading
than *reed ferelyche*, a red wonder.

17

Unless *bonk* is a collective plural, which is unlikely, *bonkes* is called
for.

18

The repetition of *with clene men of armes* is probably a scribal error. Malory, using the poem as a source, wrote at this point "sir Kay, sir Clegis, and sir Bedwere the ryche encounters with them by a clyffsyde" and acting on this evidence, one editor of the poem emends 2156 to *Sir Kayous, sir Clegis, [sir Bedevere the ryche]*.

19

A good example of incorrect word division, *a nayre and* appears in a better MS as *ane errant*.

20

Line 87 is an example of what George Kane calls a "homoeograph," a reading which preserves "something of the shape of the supplanted, original words or phrases, but little or nothing of their meaning or relation to the context." [42] Thus *wlonkes* (nobles) makes no sense, and *wonges* (cheeks) is obviously correct in context.

21

Since this scribe sometimes leaves his minim *i*'s undotted, *heui* could well be *hem*, a syntactically better reading if a pronominal subject is assumed.

22

Kane prefers *chosen hem to chaffre* to *chosen to chaffare* and to *chosen chaffare* on the grounds that it is the "harder reading" because of its "less obvious meaning 'betook, devoted themselves to' " (*Piers Plowman*, p. 159). The principle here, established by Moore (*Contributions to the Textual Criticism of the Divina Commedia* [Cambridge, 1889]), is that since scribes tend to simplify difficult constructions, the "hardest" reading of a given line may generally be regarded as the oldest.

23

The repetition of *swete* seems un-Chaucerian. Alternate MSS sup-

ply *leve* and *leef* which avoid the repetition and provide a good rhyme. The French source reads *novele*.

24

The usual reading, *north-north-west*, is a good example of a choice of readings based on meaning, the best alternatives being *north nor west* and *north(e) west*. Robinson's note states that

> This passage affords a possible clue to the date of the poem. Though Venus can never be seen exactly in the position named, she might be so described when she is at or near her greatest distance north from the equator, and the sun is about 45° east of the vernal equinox. Early in May, 1382, as Professor Koch pointed out (Chronology, pp. 37–38), she was visible as evening star slightly north of the northwest point, and Professor Manly (Morsbach Festschrift, pp. 288–89) has shown that the conditions were also fulfilled in 1374 and 1390. Of these three years, 1382 alone seems a probable time for the composition of the Parliament.
>
> Of course, as Professor Manly remarks, the phrase *north-north-west* may not have been used with exact astronomical significance. It may mean only "in an unpropitious position." He compares Hamlet's "I am but mad north-north west" (ii, 2, 396).
>
> (*The Works of Geoffrey Chaucer* [Boston, 1957], p. 793)

NOTES TO TEXTUAL CRITICISM

1. E. Talbot Donaldson, "The Psychology of Editors of Middle English Texts," *Speaking of Chaucer* (New York, 1970), 118.

2. See pp. 126ff. below.

3. John M. Manly and Edith Rickert, *The Text of the Canterbury Tales* (Chicago, 1940), II, 3–4.

4. See Vinton A. Dearing, "Methods of Textual Editing," *Bibliography and Textual Criticism*, ed. O. M. Branch, Jr., and Warner Barnes (Chicago, 1969), 84–89, for a description of a number of methods of recording variants including the Hinman collating machine and the IBM 7090.

5. See Manly and Rickert, *The Text of the Canterbury Tales*, II, 3–10, for a full description of this procedure.

6. The heading designating the unit to be compared.

7. This card contains the first half-line of a poem of doubtful origin. The MS designations reflect the libraries, either public or of private societies, in which the MSS

are presently housed, except for the MS referred to as EAP by virtue of a scrawled marginal note on its first folio. These letters are thought to have been scrawled by an unknown early owner and to stand perhaps for Early Archetype [or] Prototype. In spite of this inscription, however, the MS is unsavory, written as it is on cheap paper and stained by what chemical analysis reveals to be whiskey.

8. Usually defined as a copy or reproduction, nowadays photographic, of the MS itself.

9. Eleanor Hammond, *Chaucer: A Bibliographical Manual* (New York, 1908), 106. Italics added.

10. *Ibid.*

11. A. E. Housman, "Preface to Manilius I," *Selected Prose*, ed. Carter, 35.

12. Confusion abounds in the definitions assigned to "archetype" and "original" by the masters. Paul Maas regards the original as "a dictation revised by the author" [Maas, *Textual Criticism*, tr. Barbara Flowers (Oxford, 1958), 1] which may or may not be extant, and the archetype as the "exemplar [thus an extant MS] from which the first split originated" (*Textual Criticism*, 2). F. T. Bowers [*Encyclopedia Britannica* (1971), XXI, 919] identifies the original as the "latest immediate ancestor to all manuscripts"—just what Maas had called the archetype. James Willis enjoys the best of both worlds by defining one in terms of the other: he says that the archetype is "the common original whence all known manuscripts of a given text are derived." [James Willis, *Latin Textual Criticism* (Urbana, 1972), 227]

In this volume, "archetype" is to be interpreted as that extant MS which most nearly approaches that from which all other MSS descend, and "original" as "the text the author intended." [James Thorpe, *Principles of Textual Criticism* (San Marino, 1972), 109]

13. This definition of the object of recension seems innocent enough, but it is loaded with assumptions. Is the most primitive necessarily the "best" (and in what sense "best") or even the most "authoritative" MS? Is the purpose of emendation simply to restore the pristine form of the most primitive extant MS or to attempt to go beyond all extant MSS in search of a hypothetical Urarchetype, now lost, or even of that ultimate source, the original, the author's "intended" text?

14. See footnote 12 above. In the words of James Willis, Maas's volume is "acute and learned and almost totally useless" (p. 231), at least for editors whose MSS do not conform to Maas's carefully laid out hypotheses.

15. Maas, *Textual Criticism*, 3.

16. Donaldson, "The Psychology of Editors of Middle English Texts," 110.

17. That is, of eliminating from consideration those MSS deemed "worthless" because they depend "exclusively upon a surviving exemplar." See Maas, *Textual Criticism*, 2.

18. *Ibid.*, 7. Italics added.

19 Hammond, *Chaucer*, 109.

20. Maas, *Textual Criticism*, 8–9. Italics added.

21. More complex stemmata can be found in Bowers, *Encyclopedia Britannica*, XXI, 919ff; in Willis, *Latin Textual Criticism*, 13–34; and in L. D. Reynolds and N. G. Wilson, *Scribes and Scholar* (Oxford, 1968), 137ff.,among others. Unlike these other writers, we have (1) begun with the collation rather than with the completed chart in order to show the evolution of a typical stemma and (2) attempted to reduce the process to the simplest possible case in order to illustrate the principles involved.

22. Variants that, as defined by W. W. Greg, "affect the author's meaning or the essence of his expression," as distinct from "accidental" variants in "spelling, punctuation, word-division, and the like, affecting mainly its formal presentation" [Greg, "The Rationale of Copy-Text," *Collected Papers* (Oxford, 1966), 376]. "Indicative

errors" are those "which can be utilized to make stemmatic inferences" (Maas, *Textual Criticism*, 42) and are divisible into "separative" and "conjective" errors which serve to divide or join MS or groups of MSS.

23. Maas states in *Textual Criticism*, 42, that he meant to "ask simply what characteristics an *error* must have in order to be utilized for stemmatic purposes."

24. Donaldson, "The Psychology of Editors of Middle English Texts," 107.

25. Thorpe, *Principles of Textual Criticism*, 115.

26. Dom Henri Quentin, *Essais de Critique Textuelle* (Paris, 1926), 37.

27. Donaldson, "The Psychology of Editors of Middle English Texts," 112.

28. See Bedier's edition of *Lai de L'ombre* (Paris, 1913) and *La Tradition Manuscrite de "Lai de L'ombre"* (Paris, 1929).

29. Quoted by Manly and Rickert, *The Text of the Canterbury Tales*, 13.

30. Bowers, *Encyclopedia Britannica*, XXI, 921.

31. The following discussion, taken from Moore-Markquart, *Historical Outlines of English Sounds and Inflections* (Ann Arbor, 1960), 77–78, *n* 77, demonstrates the complexity of the matter:

The character ȝ was called ȝoȝ [jɔx], and was a slight modification of the Old English form of the letter ġ. The Old English g represented two sounds, that of [j], in dæġ, and that of [ɣ] in āgen. This latter sound is a fricative like the g of North German sagen. In Middle English the sound of [j] was preserved if it occurred at the beginning of a word, as in ȝe, from OE ġē. But when it was preceded by a vowel it united with the vowel to form a diphthong, as in ME dai from OE dæġ. The Old English sound [ɣ] became [w] in early ME when preceded by a back vowel, and then it united with the preceding vowel to form a diphthong, as in ME owen [ɔːuən] from OE āgen. In the few words in which it was followed by a vowel and preceded by a consonant, OE [ɣ] became [w] in ME, e.g., in halwien, from OE hālgian. OE initial [ɣ] however, became in ME a stop consonant like the g in Modern English good. This stop g was then spelled with a new variety of the letter g which was very much like the modern g. The Old English form of the letter g, slightly modified, as shown above, was then used to spell the sounds other than stop g which had developed out of the two Old English sounds of g. That is, it was used to represent:

1. The sound of [j], e.g., in ȝe, from OE ġē;
2. The sound of [w], e.g., in halȝien, from OE hālgian;
3. The second element of the diphthong [æɪ], e.g., in daȝ from OE dæġ and weȝ from OE weg;
4. The second element of the diphthongs [ɑu] and [ɔːu], e.g., in draȝen from OE dragan, and aȝen or oȝen from OE āgen.

It was also used to represent:

5. The sound of [x], e.g., in niȝt from OE niht.

[w] is spelled ȝ, g, h, or gh when it developed out of OE [ɣ], e.g., in halȝien, alghien from OE hālgian.

32. Willis, *Latin Textual Criticism*, 10, conjectures that 25 percent of the errors in Macrobius "would entirely escape detection if one had not other manuscripts available for comparison."

33. Housman, "Preface to Manilius I," 36.

34. Willis, *Latin Textual Criticism*, 8.

35. *Ibid.*, 9, 11.

36. Bowers, *Encyclopedia Britannica*, XXI, 919.

37. Eugene Vinaver, "Principles of Textual Emendation," *Studies in French Lan-*

guage and Medieval Literature presented to Professor M. K. Pope (Manchester, 1939), 351–69.

38. W. W. Greg, "Review of Vinaver's *Principles of Textual Emendation*," 428.

39. H. J. Chaytor, *From Script to Print: An Introduction to Medieval Vernacular Literature* (Cambridge, 1945), 19. The choice of examples for this selection has been a difficult process. Therefore, in order to illustrate as briefly and as simply as possible the kinds of problems involved, we have chosen the examples from two sources, both of which are likely to be familiar to the student of Middle English—*The Canterbury Tales* and the works of the *Pearl*-poet. The first of these illustrates very well how an editor must choose between MS readings and the second how he must occasionally reconstruct a single text.

40. The reader who is interested in compiling a compedium of possible types of errors might well examine Manly and Rickert's notes in Volumes III and IV of *The Text of the Canterbury Tales*. Willis, *Latin Textual Criticism*, 49, provides a list of possible errors arranged on slightly different principles as do Robert J. Gates, *The Awntyrs off Arthure* (Philadelphia, 1969) 53ff. and George Kane, *Piers Plowman: The A Version* (London, 1960), 115 ff.

41. Bowers, *Encyclopedia Britannica*, 919.

42. Kane, *Piers Plowman*, 132.

THE FINISHED EDITION

What here follows is meant for one only of the three classes into whose hands this book will come. It is not for those who are critics: they know it already and will find it nothing but a string of truisms. It is not for those who never will be critics: they cannot grasp it and will find it nothing but a string of paradoxes. It is for beginners; for those who are not critics yet, but are neither too dull to learn nor too self-satisfied to wish to learn.

A. E. HOUSMAN

THE finished scholarly edition generally consists of five parts: text, apparatus, glossary, notes (explanatory and/or textual), and introduction, which itself is conventionally divided into a number of parts.

I. THE PRINTED TEXT

Although the editor has at this point substantially established his text, two major editorial tasks remain in conjunction with final transcription—punctuation and typography.

The editor should remember first that styles in punctuation change and second that punctuation vitally affects meaning. He should thus be wary indeed of the kind of heavy-handed, indiscriminate sprinkling of commas and semicolons which obscure the texts of some earlier editors. And he should justify in his explanatory notes (1) any definitive punctuation made by him in passages where punctuation could vitally affect interpretation and (2) any radical changes in the punctuation of earlier editors.

One special point of punctuation needs also to be considered—the noting of expansions of abbreviations, previously mentioned briefly in conjunction with transcription. The usual practice of earlier editors was simply to italicize such expansions in the text and to list in a headnote the principal forms of abbreviations expanded by them. More recent editors are sometimes inclined to omit these

notices of expansions presumably on the grounds that either they make for a cluttered page and/or they have been noted in previous editions.

The second of these reasons seems at least partially valid, the first not at all. Since the page of a scholarly edition is at best a cluttered affair divided as it is at least into two, if not into three, sections and blemished by a variety of typefaces, one more set of italics will hardly make any aesthetic difference. If, however, expansions of abbreviations have been noted in previous editions, the editor may well feel that they are intrusions in his own, though he should consider carefully the accessibility of those earlier editions to the student. For example, there really seems little point in marking *ad nauseam* the *Gawain*-poet's abbreviations, though those of Layamon's *Brut* might be useful.

Whatever his conclusions regarding punctuation, the noting of abbreviations, and the typographical characters used,[1] the editor should supply the reader with a headnote, the fuller the better, to his text explaining carefully his practices in transcription.

One such headnote reads:

THE TEXT

THE spelling of the manuscript is reproduced, except for correction of scribal errors. Emendations are indicated by footnotes, which give the forms in the manuscript and the names of those who proposed the principal emendations adopted. No emendations have been made on purely metrical grounds, for the details of the original metrical form are too uncertain; but a few have been made to restore alliteration. Corrections made by the original scribe are as a rule not recorded. Abbreviations have been expanded without notice. There is doubt about the meaning of only three of them: 1. The sign ᵹ, which normally means -*us*, occasionally serves as a mere equivalent of -*s*; see footnotes to 456, 2027. The pronoun 'us' is written *vᵹ* everywhere except 2246, where it is once *vs*. This may be a scribal eccentricity which should be printed *vs* throughout (so Magoun, *Anglia* lxi (1937), 129–30); yet since the abbreviation certainly stands for -*us* in many places some uncertainty remains, and the word is here shown as *vus* in the usual way. 2. The compendium *wᵗ* could stand for either *with* or *wyth*, both of which are used when the word is written out; *with* has been

chosen as the simpler. 3. The crossed q, used in writing Latin for *quod*, is here expanded to *quop*. The word is nowhere so written in the manuscript, but cf. *cope* 776.

Word-division has been regularized without notice: words which stand divided in the manuscript, such as *in noȝe* 514, have been joined (one or two special collocations are hyphenated, as *as-tit* 31), and many which are written without space, such as *bisypez* 17, have been separated. The long *i* is printed *j* except in *iwis* and the pronoun *I*. The manuscript does not distinguish in form between ȝ and *z*, the form ȝ serving for both; but where the letter is *z* it is so printed. Capital letters are used as in modern English, and punctuation—which does not exist in the manuscript—is supplied. The only diacritic introduced is an acute accent to mark an unaccented *e* when it stands for etymological *i* or OFr. *é*, as in *meré* 'merry', *bewté* 'beauty'.[2]

II. THE APPARATUS

The apparatus consists of a noting, by convention at the bottoms of the pages containing the text, of textual variants. But what variants and how many? There are, of course, a number of possibilities:

(1) The very minimum would be a listing of all those forms which had appeared in the copy-text and had been replaced by the editor's emendations. The reader should always be able to reconstruct the copy-text from the apparatus.

(2) If space permits a fuller apparatus, the editor should include the significant MS readings and emendations of former editors, though here some choice of items may be necessary. The punctuation of former editors can be ignored as can their emendations which do not, in the editor's opinion, substantially differ either from the copy-text or from his own edition.

(3) Third (though second in priority to many editors) would be an inclusion of the significant variants from the principal MSS or groups of MSS as gleaned from the collation. Here again unless, like Manly and Rickert, he decides to print a complete collation, the editor must decide which MSS and which readings to include; but if by this time he does not have definite opinions on these matters, he is beyond our advice.

The actual typography of the apparatus should be carefully considered and agreed upon with the printer. The particular arrangement of typefaces (generally limited in typescript to capitals, lower case, and to underlinings—which will be translated into italics by a printer) and symbols (brackets, parentheses, colons, etc.) must communicate swiftly and accurately to the reader the precise relation of the variants to the text. And, as with the text, the editor ideally should supply an explanation, such as this one, of the principle of selection governing the apparatus and of the symbols used:

> The text is supported by a critical apparatus. This records all substantive variants from the text, all morphological variants which may possibly be substantive, the majority of grammatical variants, the majority of dialect variants, and a great many orthographical variants.
>
> The apparatus is thus unusually full, and sets out a more minute collation than is at present in favour. Several circumstances have combined to require this. First, as this introduction will have shown, the nature of the textual problem calls for the full presentation of substantive variants. A 'judicious selection,' on whatever principle, is not good enough. In addition, because in the course of *Piers Plowman* studies various theories have been supported by argument from linguistic forms, it seems advisable to record not merely substantive variants, but also linguistic variants to indicate the character of this evidence. The critical apparatus thus serves a second purpose over and above its relation to the textual problem, by exhibiting the variety of linguistic and orthographical forms to be found not merely in different manuscripts, but within individual manuscripts. Finally the nature of the problem of determining the original language of this poem must be shown; this seems best done by a certain increase in the size of an apparatus already made bulky by its other functions.
>
> The apparatus is, on the whole, set out after the conventional practice. The lemma, closed by a square bracket, is followed by its variant readings. The authority for these is shown by the sigils after them, distinct variants being set off by semicolons, and the variants for any lemma by a full stop. This use of punctuation in the apparatus, making it easier to read quickly, seems permissible because no variants of punctuation are recorded.[3]

III. THE GLOSSARY

Having established his text and apparatus, the editor should proceed to construct a glossary and a set of explanatory or non-textual notes. These two items are essential to any edition, the glossary not only as a reading aid, but more importantly as a guide to the vocabulary of the writer and as one more piece in the jigsaw of Middle English, the notes as a means of illuminating what is dark and relating what is disjointed. Glossary and notes are not simply adjuncts to the text; properly done, they are integral parts of the editor's total presentation. Neither, however, can be properly done concurrently with the textual editing, though the substance of future notes can be noted (carefully, by line number) in passing. The glossary, however, must wait upon an unalterable text lest last minute textual changes render incorrect glossary entries.

There is only one satisfactory way of compiling a glossary, on index cards, but there are a number of questions to be answered before the work can begin. First, is the glossary to include every instance of every word; is it, in short, to be a concordance as well as a glossary? Second, if it is not to include every instance, is it nonetheless to include examples of every meaning and usage (part of speech, etc.) of every word? Third, is it to include those inflected forms and variant spellings which are not critical to meaning or usage? Fourth, is it to be etymological, to include the probable derivation of every word?

The answers to these questions will depend upon the usages to which the editor feels his edition will be put and the previous history of his text. For example, if a concordance to his text already exists, there would be little point in his compiling a complete glossary, though in some instances a cross check might be useful. If no such complete glossary exists for the editor's text, one would make possible word counts and other vocabulary studies otherwise impossible.

However, no matter what one decides as to completeness of instance, every variation in meaning and usage *must* be recorded. There are all sorts of homophonic and homonymic traps in Middle English; to quote Little Buttercup, "things are seldom what they seem." *Hat* can be a head covering or a form of *to have*; *art* can be a

noun or a verb; *born* can relate to portage or to birth or to a flood. As to the inclusion of every variation in form and spelling, even by a system of cross references, the editor again must keep in mind both the use to which the glossary will be put and the linguistic sophistication of the user. The compiler of a descriptive linguistic study utilizing the edition would certainly want every variant form to be listed; the student reader not thoroughly familiar with the basic form of the word to be searched would also find such a practice desirable. However, the listing of every variant is an expensive practice and in most cases unnecessary. The editor is probably well advised to list only those variants which, while not critical to either meaning or form, nevertheless make the compilations of the linguist and the word search of the reader easier.

Etymological glossaries are of immense use and perpetual fascination. They are, however, extremely laborious to prepare and more often than not simply repeat the work of previous editions or, if nothing else, of the *New English Dictionary*, the *Middle English Dictionary*, the Wrights' *Dialect Dictionary*, and half a dozen other standard works. The editor seems well advised, therefore, to include in his explanatory notes rather than in the glossary instances in which he differs with the etymology of the standard authorities. On this last point, it is a good practice to mark with an asterisk in the glossary those words which are treated in the explanatory notes. The asterisk should logically be placed within the entry preceding the appropriate line number.

While the exact typography of the glossary entry is, like that of the apparatus, a matter finally to be settled by editor and publisher, the editor should nonetheless give the appearance of the entry some consideration even in typescript. A minimum of three type forms or faces would seem desirable—one for the entry word or words, another for the part of speech, and a third for the definition and line numbers. One is here severely limited by the typewriter keyboard, but a good practical solution might be to use capitals for the entry word, italics (underscoring) for the part of speech, and lower case for the definitions.

Whatever one chooses to include or exclude from the glossary and

however he chooses to arrange his entries, he certainly owes the reader a statement of the principles upon which the glossary is constructed, including an explanation of the kinds of information glossed and of the forms of notation used. The following specimen illustrates a well thought out and executed glossary of a multi-text edition:

GLOSSARY

THE Glossary is a complete record of the forms used in the Thornton version, but not of all occurrences of each form; where the number of occurrences is incomplete, &c. is added. Forms from the Ware text (prefixed by W) are quoted only when they show a notable linguistic (as opposed to spelling) variation, or when an odd corruption has occurred, as in W *duke pere* or *ducheperis* for *douze per(s)*. In the few instances where an entirely different word has been substituted in W, e.g. *affligid* where T has *flayede*, this is entered separately. Derivations are given only exceptionally, for unusual words or on points of special linguistic interest. An asterisk before a number reference indicates an emended form.

The following points of arrangement may be noted: ʒ follows g; þ is entered under t, with th; the initial i = j is separated from i = i; internal y = i is treated as i; initial v = u is separated from v = v; medial u = v is treated as v (e.g. *out* before *ouer*).

Abbreviations which may not be obvious are: AF., Anglo-French; E., English; F., French; (med.) L., (Medieval) Latin; LG., Low German; MDu., Middle Dutch; MHG., Middle High German; MLG., Middle Low German; N., North(ern); Nth., Northumbrian; OF., Old French; ONF., the Northern dialects of Old French; Sc., Scottish; n. = see Note; *MED.*, A Middle English Dictionary (in preparation, ed. H. Kurath and S. M. Kuhn); *OED.*, The Oxford English Dictionary.

A

a *indef. art. a* 4, 7, 23 &c; an(c) reg. before *b*, 5, 25, 84, &c.

abaschede *pt. s.* took by surprise, confounded 369; W basshed.

abyde, habyde *v. intr.* to stay, remain, endure 536, 583, 631; abydes *pr. 3 s.* stays, waits 360; habade *pt. s.* lingered 7.

about *adv.* all round, all over 93;

aboute, abowte about, round, here and there 46, 76 &c.

adversarye *n.* adversary 311.

affligid *pp.* afflicted, distressed W 428.

affrayede *pt. s.* alarmed, frightened 356.

aftir(e) *adv.* afterwards, then 74, 277, 294, &c.; aftir(e), aftyr

prep. after, in pursuit of 63, 226, &c.; after 332, 379, &c.; W aftur.

agayne *adv.* again 437; W ayayn.

age *n.* age 164.

agreed *pt. s. refl.* agreed 358.

ay *adv.* always, ever 564; W hay.

ayers *n. pl.* heirs 577; W heyris.

ayther(e) *adj.* either 28, each 512; *pron.* both 456. [OE. *ǣgþer*; see ouþer]

aldeste see Olde.

alle *adj.* all 49, 149, 177. &c.; *adv.* entirely 26, 119, 122, &c; ~ *by-dene*, see by-dene.

alle *n.* all, everything, everyone 57, 92, 184, &c.

als *conj.* as (when, while) 3, 7, 21, &c.; (even) as, like 47, 65, 114, &c.; *adv.* (just) as 271; also 144. See as.

also *adv.* also, as well 167, 511.

amatistes *n. pl.* amethists 127.

amen *interj.* Amen 665.

amende *pr. subj. 3 s.* restore, convert [4]

The three following headnotes illustrate various other ways of handling glossaries, depending on the use to which the editor feels the glossary will be put. The first is to what seems to be a school edition:

GLOSSARY

This is a glossary of words which may give difficulty to the reader, and is designed solely for the needs of the text. It does not aim to repeat explanations already given in the notes. Alphabetical order is normal, except that initial *y* as past participle prefix is ignored.[5]

The other two are parts of works intended for scholars:

GLOSSARY

The Glossary includes all words in the text and the variants, with their etymologies, except for words common in ME (including articles, prepositions and personal pronouns) and words which have essentially the same form and meaning in both ME and ModE. Regularly inflected forms of nouns and weak verbs are not usually listed separately, and frequently occurring items are curtailed and marked *etc.*

All forms of a word are placed under the entry for MS D, which will usually be the most common spelling of the word if there are more than one. The head-word for verbs is the infinitive or present tense, unless neither occurs, in which case the form will be specified (*pt.* = preterite, *pr.p.* = present participle, etc.). Line numbers without an identifying letter indicate MS D, and the form may or may not also occur in the other MSS.

In the alphabetical arrangement *th* and *þ*, *u* and *v*, *i* and vocalic *y* are not distinguished. ȝ follows *g*.[6]

GLOSSARY

In the Glossary completeness is aimed at. Intentional exceptions are: (i) references to common forms or uses have been much curtailed (marked *etc.*); (ii) variation between ȝ, *gh*; *i*, *y*; *th*, *þ*; *u*, *v*; and final *-es*, *-ez*, has often been disregarded; (iii) the inflected forms of nouns, adjectives, and weak verbs have only exceptionally been recorded (for their normal forms see pp. 143–7).

Etymologies. These are given as an aid in interpreting spellings, fixing meanings, and differentiating words of diverse origin and similar appearance. Though extremely brief, they are not solely repetitions of common material; several are here (often very tentatively) suggested for the first time, e.g. *burde*, *misy*, *rupe*, *schynder*, *wone*. For the better illustration of the forms of the text, the Old French forms cited are largely Anglo-Norman (usually without specification), the Old English forms Anglian. The marking of long vowels has not been attempted in Old French. In Old English the long vowels are marked as in *ān*; uncertain quantity or probable shortening in the Old English period is marked as in ARE, *ær*; vowels lengthened in Old English (e.g., before *ld*) are marked as in BOLD, *báld*, when the forms of the text point to, or allow of the possibility of, this lengthening. On the forms cited from Old Norse see pp. 140–1; long vowels are marked as in *ár*.

Arrangement. In Glossary and Index of Names (i) ȝ has a separate alphabetical place immediately after g; (ii) þ has a separate place immediately after t, and here also is included rare initial th; (iii) the MS. distinction between initial u, v, and i, j has not been observed—only v and i are used; (iv) initially y has its usual place, but medially and finally it will be found in the alphabetical place of i.[7]

A number of recent editions, especially those intended for classroom use,[8] have printed their glossaries directly under the passages which they gloss. While such a practice is extremely convenient to the student who must otherwise refer to the "back of the book," it nevertheless occasions what seem to be unanswerable questions and hence arbitrary answers. How many times shall a term be glossed: only once (in which case the forgetful student will never find its definition upon encountering its second use), each time it appears (a prohibitively expensive practice), or some arbitrary number (sev-

enty times seven has biblical sanction)? In general, the "back of the book," while inconvenient, seems the best place for the glossary.

IV. NOTES

The notes to an edition fall rather obviously into two categories whether or not they are actually so separated: textual and explanatory. Textual notes should be essentially amplifications of the apparatus. They provide the editor an opportunity to justify emendations which might appear radical to the reader. Explanatory notes, on the other hand, cover a variety of matters. Although a comprehensive, carefully-prepared set of explanatory notes is, aside from the establishment of a hitherto unprocurable text, the greatest gift an editor can bestow upon a reader, it is generally compiled without any consideration whatsoever of the needs of the recipient. One too often finds a "galley" noted as an "ancient ship propelled by sails and oars" while the most abstruse medieval nautical term is given a brief notice in the glossary.

It would seem obvious that what needs noting, either in textual or interpretative matters, are (1) those items which differ from the routine practices of the poet, for example his sudden use of an obscure construction or word, (2) those places in the text which demand "background" information (the poet's allusion to a particular convention of courtly love) or which show the influence of another writer or of a genre in either content or style (the use of the dream vision); (3) lines or passages which affect the internal organization and the interpretation of the work, repeated images, structural units, and the like, and a frequently forgotten category (4) those items which have in notes and previous editions assumed the status of cruces, *loci classici*, (the "hyȝ seysoun" in *Pearl* or the "preestes thre" of the General Prologue).

A sample from Tolkien and Gordon's second edition of *Sir Gawain and the Green Knight* demonstrates the range of a good set of notes:

1814 *þat lufsum vnder lyne.* 'That lovely one under linen' is a kind of kenning for 'that lovely lady'. There were many such conventional phrases describing persons as 'fair under garment'. This same one occurs in *Sir Tristrem* 1202, 2816; *Eger and Grime* (in the Percy Folio MS., ed. J. W. Hales and F. J. Furnivall (London, 1867)) 251; and, applied to lords, in *Emaré* 864. Some

of the parallel phrases are: 'worthy under wede', 'semely under serke', *Emaré* 250, 501; 'geynest under gore', 'brihtest under bys', *Harley Lyrics* (ed. Brook) 4. 37, 5. 38; 'comelye under kell', *The Green Knight* (Percy Folio) 255.

1832–3 *schaped* is best derived from *chape*, a metal mount or trimming. *M.E.D.* quotes some examples of the noun spelt *schape*, and cf. *schere* for *chere* 334. The adj. appears in Chaucer, *Canterbury Tales, Prol. 366:* 'Hir knyves were chaped noght with bras, But al with silver.' For *brayden* used of gold cf. especially *Purity* 1481 'brayden of golde', and for *beten* of gold applied to fabric *Beues of Hamtoun* (ed. E. Kölbing, E.E.T.S.E.s. xlvi (1885)) 1159: 'þe broider is of tuli selk, Beten abouten wiþ rede gold.'

1836 *nay* 'said . . . not' is the past tense of *nie*, unrecorded in the present, but from the stressed stem *ni-* of OFr. *neier*. The past is formed on the analogy of *lie/lay*. It occurs again in *Purity* 805: 'And þay nay þat þay nolde neȝ no howsez' (Napier). Elsewhere the verb is *nay*, past *nayed* (see *O.E.D.*).

1853 *hapel vnder heuen*. Cf. OE. 'hæleð under heofonum', as *Beowulf* 52, *Solomon and Saturn* (ed. Menner (New York, 1941)) 60. Probably the ME. phrase descends from this; it occurs again in *Wars Alex.* 4937.

1859 *þulged*. Though this form occurs nowhere else, derivation from O.E. *ge-þyldgian* (so *O.E.D.*, but with reserve) is like that of *mynged* 1422 from *myndgian*. *Ming* is quite common, and rhymes with *sing* etc.; its *-ng* must therefore represent /ŋg/. For the development see d'Ardenne, *Iuliene*, glossary under *studgi* and p. 167.

1862 *disceuer*. The spelling with *c* before *e* may suggest that the word could be 'dissever' rather than 'discover'. But 'dissever' would have to be followed by *from*, and there are several other records of *disceuer* 'discover' in ME. (*M.E.D.* under *discoveren*); this gives better sense here. It is noteworthy that the lady does not impose the condition of secrecy until Gawain has accepted the girdle.

The exact position of the notes is again a matter to be decided between editor and publisher. There is no doubt that the notes, the textual ones certainly, are best printed on the page where the passages in the text to which they refer appear. One regrets the

relegation, occasioned by a necessary economy, of "footnotes" to the back of the book, in spite of the fact that one can now count on having more text than notes per page. A worthwhile compromise is to print the textual notes, provided they are not unduly voluminous, along with the text and the explanatory notes as a group immediately preceding the glossary. Again, the editor should take pains to mark in the glossary those items discussed in either set of notes.

V. THE INTRODUCTION

The "Introduction" to the scholarly edition should be no more and no less than its name implies: it should discuss, in narrative form, the broad, general issues[9]—textual, historical, literary, linguistic— which the reader can use to frame his own "reading" of the poem; it should not, contrary to some recent editions by scholars who should know better, itself be either startlingly original or interpretative. One cannot even estimate the critical harm done to a major writer by what is at absolute best an idiosyncratic interpretation of his work contained in the introduction in what must for years to come of economic necessity be its definitive edition.

The usual introduction tends to fall into the following sections: The Manuscript, Date and Authorship, Historical and Literary Backgrounds, Literary Qualities, Special Problems, Language, and Bibliography.

A. *The Manuscript*

Both the physical appearance and contents of the manuscript should here be described in reasonable detail; as always, questions of judgment and taste must certainly determine the individual items to be included. It would seem profitable to no one to list every instance of the scribe's writing around a tear in the vellum, but to record every change in the ownership of the MS might indeed be helpful.

B. *Date and Authorship*

While the length of this section will depend upon the relative importance of date and authorship to the work at hand, there are a few principles worth noting which apply to the whole introduction. First, the editor should review carefully and succinctly the impor-

tant theories as to both date and authorship. There is nothing more useful to the reader than an organized review of research. The editor can provide a real service here by grouping individual critics into critical schools. Second, the editor should restrict cautiously his own judgments on these matters, no matter how strong his feelings. If he *must* express himself, he should do so in a journal article; he should not take advantage of his editorial position to be original. He may, however, without taking sides himself, summarize what seems to be the consensus of scholars. The date and authorship section might well include discussions, where appropriate, of such related items as the place of the work in the author's canon and the motivation and circumstances of its composition.

C. Historical and Literary Backgrounds

Here is the place where the editor may well expend the creative energy he has so far been admonished to curb. "The Alliterative Revival," "Courtly Love," "The Dream Vision," "The Peasant's Revolt," "The Rise of the Medieval Lyric," "Fourteenth Century Mysticism"—all manner of topics here demand the editor's best organizational skills and his best prose. The virtues to be striven for are inclusiveness (which is not quite the same as completeness), conciseness (which is not quite the same as brevity), and relevance to the work at hand. The editor should remember that his work will probably not be consulted by the student in search of a standard essay on a general topic, but by one who wishes that background knowledge which will directly assist him in reading a particular work. Thus the introductory essay on the dream vision should demonstrate its use in *Pearl* and mention only in passing, if at all, *The Book of the Duchess*.

D. Literary Qualities

Such topics as versification, imagery, figures of speech, and rhyme immediately suggest themselves. Again the editor should restrict himself to what is pertinent to the work at hand.

E. Special Problems

While not appropriate to every edition, the editor will certainly

need to consider any special kinds of topics demanded by his work—a stage history, for example, in the case of a play; the writer's influence on subsequent writers in that of *Piers Plowman* or Chaucer; a detailed source examination in that of Malory.

F. *Language*

Most editions of Middle English works contain rather specialized discussions of the poets' language or dialect. Such sections generally presume a working knowledge of Middle English so that the editor feels within his rights when he states that his poet's language is "more advanced than that of London" or that it "contains many northerly features." Non-linguistic features such as geography, biography, or poetics which help identify the poet's dialect may well be included here.

G. *Bibliography*

Several choices are available to the bibliographer: (1) a complete bibliography, (2) a bibliography of sources cited in the introduction and/or notes, (3) a "selected" bibliography (the principle of selection depending upon the prospective audience and use of the edition), or, what one usually finds, (4) a random assortment of what the editor happens to have read. The immediate rejection of choices 1 and 4 is recommended on the grounds that 1 is impossible and 4 misleading. In choosing between 2 and 3, there are several factors to consider. If one chooses 2, for example, the bibliography of sources cited, or if one is sure that 3 contains all of 2, then he can avoid full bibliographical citation in the introduction and notes simply by referring the reader in his headnotes to the bibliography. If, however, his principle of selection in 3 restricts him to important works, he cannot very well list in his bibliography the type of short "Notes and Queries" items he has frequently included in his own notes and hence must cite them in full there. On the other hand, the general student consulting the bibliography frequently cannot tell by title alone—"Some New Light on Juliana of Norwich," for example— whether the article referred to is a major interpretation or a collection of brief etymological notes. One possible solution is to restrict the bibliography to general interpretative works and to cite at its first

appearance only, whether in the introduction or notes, any other items.

If at all possible, the general bibliography should be divided into categories geared to the introduction—e.g. "The Manuscript," "The Text," "Date," "Authorship," "Courtly Love," etc.—rather than into the standard "primary" and "secondary" source divisions. And if space, which is to say money, permits, the bibliography should be annotated. No more than a single sentence, or phrase, is required, but:

> Chapman, C. O. "Chaucer and the Gawain-Poet; A Conjecture," *Modern Language Notes*, LXVIII (1953), 521–24. Compares the narrative in the first part of the Squire's Tale with *Gawain*, revealing a number of points of agreement in the order of events and the conduct of the characters . . .

is surely preferable to a simple bibliographical listing, which in this case would be a puzzling one.

In the course of putting together this volume, a number of vital issues have been forgotten or neglected. We should thus like to conclude by mentioning one matter—publication—which may not seem vital to the editor at the beginning of his labors, but as his work progresses will become more and more enticing and hence more and more important.

There is only one way to find a publisher—active solicitation. The world will not beat a path to the door of the editor of a new edition of *The Pistill of Susan*. The editor should thus begin by querying the directors (start at the top!) of the university presses who have hitherto published in the field. If he can find out through company gossip (press representatives at scholarly meetings are sometimes knowledgeable) which presses are searching for what kinds of things, well and good, but generally speaking he should write anyway. His letter, which should be less than a single typewritten page, should (1) briefly describe the need and market for the volume (recent scholarly attention, only edition out of print; libraries, individual scholars, some textbook), (2) list its parts (text, notes, glossary, etc.), and (3) state its length in typescript. Should he be encouraged to submit his manuscript, he should

send it off promptly and in the cleanest possible condition. Perfect condition is not required, but perfect legibility is. And let him submit to only one press at a time.

His work will, if normal procedures are followed, first be "house read" at the press and, if it passes this test, then be sent off to be judged by one or more independent experts, who will either (1) advise the press to reject the MS, (2) advise them to accept it without alteration, or (3) advise acceptance with revision.

Since we have begun every chapter with Housman, it would be a shame not to let him have the final word, though in a different mode:

> So here are things to think on
>   That ought to make me brave,
> As I strap on for fighting
>   My sword that will not save.

NOTES TO THE FINISHED EDITION

1. See p. 55 of this volume.
2. J. R. R. Tolkien and E. V. Gordon, *Sir Gawain and the Green Knight*, 2nd ed. Norman Davis (Oxford, 1967).
3. George Kane, ed., *Piers Plowman: The A Version* (London, 1960), 170. A sample line and its apparatus reads:

Vndir a brood bank be a bourn[e] side,

   8 Vndir] Vnderneth J; Opon W. bourne] burne RDChVHLKWM; bournis TUH²E (*a caret below* ur T); broke J. side] brymme L.

4. M. Y. Offord, ed., *The Parlement of the Three Ages* (London, 1959).
5. Elizabeth Salter and Derek Pearsall, eds., *Piers Plowman* (Evanston, 1969).
6. Robert J. Gates, ed., *The Awntyrs off Arthure at the Terne Wathelyne* (Philadelphia, 1969).
7. Tolkien and Gordon, *Sir Gawain and the Green Knight*.
8. For example, *Chaucer's Major Poetry*, ed. A. C. Baugh (New York, 1963).
9. Particular items should be left to the notes.

BIBLIOGRAPHY

I. PALAEOGRAPHY

B[rown], T[homas], J[ulian]. "Palaeography," *Encyclopedia Britannica*, 1971. A good historical survey.

Denholm-Young, N. *Handwriting in England and Wales*. Cardiff, 1964. A series of brief, informative chapters on such items as "The History of Palaeography," "Court Hands," "Localization," etc. Worth consulting always on specifically British MSS. Thirty-one selective plates.

Johnson, Charles and Hilary Jenkinson. *English Court Hand: A.D. 1066 to 1500*, 2 vols. London, 1915. Wider in scope than the title would suggest, Vol. I (Text) particularly valuable for illustrations of individual letters, Vol. II for oversized plates.

Parkes, M. B. *English Cursive Book Hands*. Oxford, 1969.

Tannenbaum, Samuel A. *The Handwriting of the Renaissance*. New York, 1930. Though concerned with later hands, the general chapters and the large number of letter forms given make this work indispensable.

Thompson, Sir Edward Maunde. *An Introduction to Greek and Latin Palaeography*. Oxford, 1912. The standard work, largely organized around detailed discussions of 250 facsimiles.

Ullman, B. L. *Ancient Writing and its Influence*. New York, 1963. A good general primer through the advent of printing, written as a part of a series called "Our Debt to Greece and Rome." Twenty-six clearly defined plates.

Wright, C. E. *English Vernacular Hands from the Twelfth to the Thirteenth Centuries* [sic]. Oxford, 1960. A collection of twenty-four MS pages with descriptions and transcriptions. The introduction contains a short survey of the handwriting of the period.

II. MIDDLE ENGLISH

Baugh, Albert C. *A History of the English Language*. 2nd ed. New York, 1957. Long a standard work, Chapters 6 and 7 offer a comprehensive treatment of the place of Middle English in the development of the language.

Brunner, Karl. *An Outline of Middle English Grammar*. tr. Grahame Johnston. Cambridge, Mass., 1963. A briefer handbook than the Wrights', though equally convenient and useful.

Jones, Charles. *An Introduction to Middle English*. New York, 1972. Based upon "hypothetical assumptions . . . of the transformational-generative models of syntax and phonology."

Mossé, Fernand. *A Handbook of Middle English*. tr. James A. Walker. Baltimore, 1952. A grammar, plus linguistically selected texts, notes, and glossary.

Stratmann, Francis Henry. *A Middle-English Dictionary*. rev. Henry Bradley. Oxford, 1891. Though certainly not exhaustive, the best of the short dictionaries.

Wright, Joseph and Elizabeth Merry Wright. *An Elementary Middle English Grammar*. London, 1923. As its preface states, a "concise account of the phonology and inflexions of the Middle English period."

III. TEXTUAL CRITICISM

Bowers, Fredson. "Textual Criticism," *The Aims and Methods of Scholarship in Modern Languages and Literature*. New York, 1963. A condensed and straightforward treatment of the subject.

———. "Textual Criticism," *Encyclopedia Britannica*, 1971. A good overview.

Brack, O. M., Jr. and Warner Barnes, eds. *Bibliography and Textual Criticism*. Chicago, 1969. An anthology containing the best of Greg, Bowers, Dearing, Thorpe, Todd, and others, but treating only printed texts.

Chaytor, H. J. *From Script to Print: An Introduction to Medieval Vernacular Literature*. Cambridge, 1945. An interesting inquiry into medieval publication, especially as regards scribal habits.

Clark, A. C. *The Descent of Manuscripts*. Oxford, 1918. Though devoted to specific classical problems, the "Preface" contains some generalized principles.

D'Ardenne, Simonne R. T. O. "The Editing of Middle English Texts," *English Studies Today*. Oxford, 1951. A whimsical dialogue.

Dearing, Vinton A. *A Manual of Textual Analysis*. Berkeley, 1959. Though statistically oriented and principally involved with printed texts, well worth consulting.

Donaldson, E. Talbot. "The Psychology of Editors of Middle English Texts," *Speaking of Chaucer*. New York, 1970. A corrective to much that has been written about the mysteries of textual criticism.

Greg, W. W. *The Calculus of Variants*. Oxford, 1927. Much praised, highly technical account of Greg's system of establishing a genealogy of MSS by mathematical principles.

———. *The Collected Papers of Sir Walter W. Greg*. ed. J. C. Maxwell. Oxford, 1966. A good selection including "The Rationale of Copy-Text."

Ham, Edward B. "Textual Criticism and Common Sense," *Romance Philology*. XII, 3 (February, 1959), 198–215. Contains a useful bibliography,

mostly of foreign articles.

Housman, A. E. *Selected Prose*. ed. John Carter. Cambridge, 1961. The most convenient introduction to the textual criticism of the greatest of all textual critics.

Kane, George. *Piers Plowman: The A Version*. London, 1960. A complex description of the harrowing problems involved in editing the MSS of the poem.

Maas, Paul. *Textual Criticism*. tr. Barbara Flower. Oxford, 1958. Brief cogent statement of the basic principles of emendation.

Manly, John M. and Edith Rickert. *The Text of the Canterbury Tales*. Vol. II. Chicago, 1940. Invaluable for advice on collation.

McKerrow, Ronald B. *An Introduction to Bibliography for Literary Students*. Oxford, 1927. The standard work for printed texts.

Reynolds, L. D. and N. G. Wilson. *Scribes and Scholars: A Guide to the Transmission of Greek and Latin Literature*. London, 1968. Chapter 5 deals with basic principles.

Thorpe, James. *Principles of Textual Criticism*. San Marino, Calif., 1972. A collection of essays dealing mostly with printed texts.

Vinaver, Eugene. "Principles of Textual Emendation," *Studies in French Language and Mediaeval Literature presented to Professor Mildred K. Pope*. Manchester, 1939, pp. 351–69. Bases principles of emendation on knowledge of scribal habits.

Willis, James. *Latin Textual Criticism*. Urbana, Ill., 1972. An excellent survey "of the many ways in which scribes were accustomed to make mistakes."

INDEX